101 FUN FOODS TO MAKE

Judy Ridgway
Illustrated by Gillian Chapman

First published in Great Britain in 1982 by
The Hamlyn Publishing Group Limited

This edition published in 1989 by
Treasure Press
Michelin House
81 Fulham Road
London SW3 6RB

ISBN 1 85051 393 7

Printed in Yugoslavia

Contents

10 **Cook's Code**
10 Safety First
10 Do's and Don'ts in the Kitchen
11 How to Follow the Recipes
12 Measuring
12 Basic Equipment

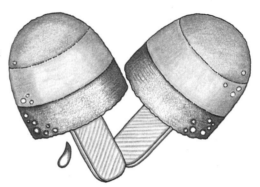

13 **First Time Cook**
14 Thousand Island Soup
15 Spicy Yoghurt Cup
16 Favourite Marmalade Sandwiches
17 Fishy Sandwich Spread
18 Growing Your Own Salad
20 Chinese Chop Suey Salad
21 Mouse Family
22 Ham Roly-poly Surprise
24 Humpty Dumpty Salad
26 Family Portrait Biscuits
28 Caribbean Trifle
29 Banana Milk Shake
30 Lime and Lemon Ice Cream Soda
31 Striped Lollies

32 **No-cook Savouries**
33 Greek Yoghurt Soup
34 Tuna Bunwiches
35 Rabbit Biscuits
36 Savoury Pinwheels
37 Cheesy Fish
38 Surprise French Loaf
40 Viking Ship
42 Mimosa Salad
43 Water Lily Salads
44 Bunch of Grapes Salad
46 Austrian Salad
48 Sunshine Salad
49 Marigold Heads
50 Salad Kebabs
52 Stuffed Eggs

53 **Teatime Treats**
54 Coconut Mountains
55 American Muffins
56 Banana Tea Bread
58 Herb Bread
59 Johnny Bread
60 Biscuit Cake
62 Initial Biscuits
63 Rock Buns
64 Artist's Cake
66 Shortbread Alphabet
67 Soda Bread
68 St. Nicholas Biscuits
70 Chocolate Butterfly Cakes
72 Hot Cross Buns
74 Gingerbread Catherine Wheels

76 **Hot Meals and Snacks**
77 Cheese, Onion and Potato Pie
78 Creamy Spinach Crunch
79 Porcupine Stew
80 Salmon Owls
82 Melting Moments
83 Sausage Cannon
84 Burgermasters' Council
86 Fisherman's Parcels
87 Potato Celeste
88 Savoury Drumsticks
89 Ploughman's Savoury Pudding
90 Corn Dog Stew
92 Canadian Pasties
94 Noughts and Crosses Pizza
96 Savoury Nests

98 Popular Puddings
99 Home-made Summer Fruit Ice Cream
100 Orange Crunch Creams
101 Gooseberry Layer Sundae
102 Ice Cream Sandwiches
104 Ice Cream Nosegay
105 Knickerbocker Glory
106 Ice Cream Clown
108 Clock Pudding
110 Yoghurt Picture Puddings
111 Fruit Crumble Pudding
112 Caramel Pears
113 Marie Antoinette Cake-and-apple Pudding
114 Apricot Cheesecake
116 Chocolate Log

117 Party Time
118 Train Salad
120 Sausage Rolls
121 Snowy Mountain Dip
122 Rower's Boat Race Dip
124 Cheese and Herb Straws
126 Cowes Regatta
128 Party Hedgehogs
129 Tomato Cocktail
130 Junior Pimms
131 Blackcurrant Punch
132 Savoury Sandwich Cake
134 Ice Cream Cabin
136 Spring Butterfly Cake
138 Castle Cake

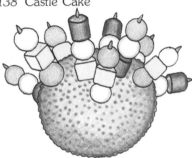

140 Home-made Sweet Shop
141 Orange and Chocolate Truffles
142 Coconut Coffee Bonbons
143 Cream Cheese Mints
144 Stuffed Date Traffic Lights
145 Peppermint Creams
146 Marzipan Fruit Basket
148 Cream Cheese and Fruit Balls
149 Date and Nut Footballs
150 Sugar Animal Zoo
152 Coconut Puffs
153 Coconut Ice
154 Nut Truffles
155 Chocolate Cheese Truffles
156 Easter Eggs

Cook's Code

Safety First

Cooking is great fun but the kitchen can be a dangerous place if you are not careful. Safety first in the kitchen is very important, so always remember to follow these few simple rules.

1. **Never** start to cook without a grown-up nearby to help you.

2. **Never** touch the cooker or any electrical equipment without permission.

3. **Always** ask a grown-up to pre-heat the oven and to take dishes in and out for you.

4. **Always** be very careful when using knives. An ordinary dinner knife will be sharp enough for most jobs.

5. **Always** shut cupboards and drawers after taking out pots and pans and utensils – it's easy to bump into things which are not properly shut.

6. **Always** wipe up spills as soon as they occur, so nobody slips on them.

Do's and Don'ts in the Kitchen

Do's

- Always wash your hands before starting to cook.

- Tie back long hair.

- Wear an apron to keep your clothes clean.

- Use a chopping board for cutting up fruit and vegetables – **never** the counter or table top.

- Sift flour and icing sugar before using them.

- Keep your working area as tidy as possible, clearing up as you go along.

- Wash up everything after you have finished and leave the kitchen clean and tidy.

- Work quickly on recipes using ice cream.

Don'ts

- Don't allow pets in the kitchen when you are cooking.

- Don't guess at weights and measures – follow the recipe and measure carefully.

- Don't handle food too much.

How to Follow the Recipes

Once you have decided what to cook it is very important to follow the recipe carefully. Start by reading all the instructions and following the drawings all the way through to the end. With each recipe is a list of the food which is to be used and how much will be needed.

When you have read the recipe to the end, get out all the ingredients. Line them up on your working surface in the order in which they are going to be used. If you do this you will be unlikely to forget or leave anything out of the ingredients. Always wash fresh fruit and vegetables, if they don't have to be peeled.

Next check the equipment which will be needed and assemble all that as well. Remember to get out the scales for solid measures (flour, sugar, etc.) and the measuring jug for liquid measures (milk, water, etc.)

If the recipe suggests asking a grown-up to open a can, to cook any of the ingredients such as hard boiling eggs, to set the oven or to help you in any other way, now is the time to ask.

When you have got everything together you will be ready to start. Carefully follow the method described in the recipe and stick to the order given. Check with the drawings to see that what you are making looks roughly the same as the illustration at each stage.

Measuring

Using scales:
Scales are used for measuring dry ingredients like flour, sugar and rice. They are also used for solid ingredients like butter and margarine.

You may sometimes need to weigh runny foods like syrup or honey. Ask for help to do this. Place the mixing bowl on the scales first. Make a note of the weight and work out what the weight should be when the correct amount of the runny food has been added. Now add the food until the indicator shows the correct weight.

Using spoons:
For small quantities of dry ingredients, a tablespoon can be used in place of the scales. A rounded tablespoon of flour or sugar is approximately equal to 25g. A rounded spoon is one where the level of the food above the edge of the spoon is the same as that below.

Quite a lot of recipes call for level tablespoons or teaspoons. Here the level of the food should be the same as that of the edge of the spoon. An easy way to make sure that a spoonful is really level is to run the straight edge of a knife across the spoon so any extra falls off.

Using measuring jugs:
Place the measuring jug on a flat surface and fill up to the level you need. Do not hold the jug in your hand as you may tilt it and not get the right amount.

Units:
Only metric units are used in this book, but here are some equivalents in imperial units in case you need them. Liquids are measured in millilitres (ml). There are 1000ml in a litre and a litre is 1·75 pints. Solids are weighed in grams (g) and 28g are equal to an ounce. Some ingredients are measured by size and 2·5 centimetres (cm) are equal to an inch.

Basic Equipment

Commonly used items in the book:

wire cooling rack

scales

bun tray

basins

baking tins

rolling pin

wooden spoons

mixing bowls

soup bowl

measuring jug

wire whisk

sieve

pastry brush

pastry cutters

fish slice

ice cream scoop

grater

lemon squeezer

First Time Cook

Thousand Island Soup

You will need:

Food:
3 sticks celery
4cm piece cucumber
2 tomatoes
2 spring onions (optional)
600ml tomato juice
juice of $\frac{1}{2}$ lemon
$\frac{1}{2}$ teaspoon Worcestershire Sauce
2–3 sprigs parsley

This makes enough for four people

Equipment:
knife
soup tureen or large bowl
measuring jug
lemon squeezer
dessertspoon

2 Measure the tomato juice using the jug. Squeeze the lemon juice and add to the jug with the Worcestershire Sauce. Stir with the spoon.

3 Pour the tomato juice over the vegetables in the tureen and place in the fridge for one hour to chill. Just before serving, break the parsley into very small pieces and sprinkle over the soup.

1 Chop the celery, cucumber, tomato and spring onion (if you decide to use it) very finely. Place the chopped vegetables in the soup tureen.

Spicy Yoghurt Cup

You will need:

Food:
150g plain yoghurt
1 level teaspoon celery salt
$\frac{1}{2}$ level teaspoon paprika pepper
black pepper
pinch mixed spices
500ml milk
2–3 sprigs parsley

This makes four cups of Spicy Yoghurt

Equipment:
basin
wooden spoon
wire whisk
knife

2 Add the milk and beat the mixture with a wire whisk. Pour out into four cups and place in the fridge to chill for one hour.

3 Very finely chop the parsley and sprinkle over the cups before serving.

1 Place the yoghurt in a basin and add the salt, pepper and spices. Mix well together.

15

Favourite Marmalade Sandwiches

You will need:

Food:
50g butter
2 tablespoons marmalade
8 slices bread

This makes 16 triangular Sandwiches

Equipment:
basin
tablespoon
knife

2 Mix the butter and marmalade together until they form a smooth paste.

3 Divide the spread into four portions and spread each portion on a slice of bread.

1 Place the butter in a basin and add the marmalade.

4 Top with the remaining slices of bread and cut across from corner to corner to make four triangles out of each round.

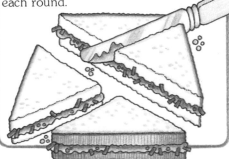

Fishy Sandwich Spread

You will need:

Food:
one 124g can sardines in tomato sauce
75g cream cheese
1 tablespoon lemon juice
salt and pepper

This is enough for six whole rounds of Fishy Sandwiches

Equipment:
fork
basin
tablespoon

Before you start, ask a grown-up to open the can of sardines.

2 Add the cream cheese, lemon juice and salt and pepper and mix again until a smooth paste is formed.

1 Tip the sardines and the tomato sauce into a basin and mash well together.

Serving idea

Instead of using sandwiches, toast eight slices of bread and spread on the fishy filling while the toast is still warm. Cut each slice into three fingers and decorate with a little cress.

Growing Your Own Salad

You will need:

Food:
1 teaspoon mustard and cress seed
1 dessertspoon mung beans
1 dessertspoon whole lentils

This will make three jars full of salad shoots

Equipment:
3 empty 450g jam jars
3 pieces of muslin about 12cm × 12cm
3 rubber bands

2 Fill the jars through the muslin with cold water. Shake the jars and tip up to allow the water to drain out through the muslin.

1 Start in the morning and place each different kind of seed in its own jar. Cover with muslin and slip on a rubber band to keep the muslin in place.

3 Fill the jars with cold water again, shake and drain. Wait for all the water to drain away and then leave the jars lying on their sides with the muslin end just a little lower than the base. A plate rack on the draining board is a good place to leave the jars.

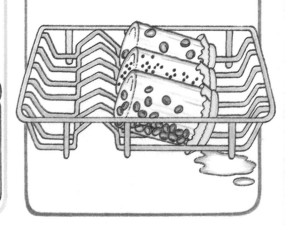

4 In the evening fill the jars with cold water again. Drain and leave tipped on their sides.

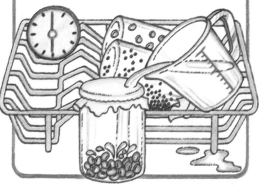

5 For the next four or five days fill the jars with cold water every morning and every evening, draining off the water each time.

6 The mustard and cress will have long enough shoots after 4–5 days, the mung beans after 5–6 days and the lentils after 5–6 days.

7 When the shoots are ready, remove the rubber bands and the muslin from the jars and take out the shoots. Use at once or store in a container in the fridge.

8 Make sure that the jars are well drained every time you fill them with water and don't forget any of the watering times!

19

Chinese Chop Suey Salad

You will need:

Food:
100g white cabbage
2 carrots
$\frac{1}{2}$ small green pepper
100g ham or cooked chicken
100g homegrown mung bean shoots
2 tablespoons salad cream or
  mayonnaise

This makes enough for four people

Equipment:
knife and fork
bowl

1 Very finely chop the cabbage and carrot into strips and place in a large bowl.

2 Remove the seeds and white parts from the green pepper and cut the green part into long thin strips and add to the salad bowl.

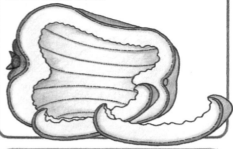

3 Cut the ham or cooked chicken into strips about the same size as the strips of pepper and add to the salad with the bean shoots and salad cream or mayonnaise.

4 Toss the salad with a fork and serve at once.

20

Mouse Family

You will need:

Food:
4 hard boiled eggs, shelled
4 slices salami or luncheon meat
1 sprig parsley
8 currants
small pieces of cheese
cress

This makes a family of four mice

Equipment:
knife

1 Cut a thin slice off the side of each egg so that they will sit firmly on a board or plate without rolling about.

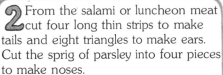

2 From the salami or luncheon meat cut four long thin strips to make tails and eight triangles to make ears. Cut the sprig of parsley into four pieces to make noses.

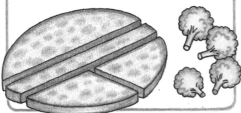

3 Cut slits at the pointed end of the eggs and insert the ears and noses. Use currants to make the eyes. Cut another slit at the other end and insert the tails.

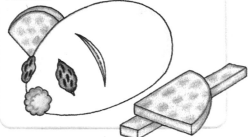

4 Place the egg mice on a dark coloured plate and decorate with small pieces of cheese and cress.

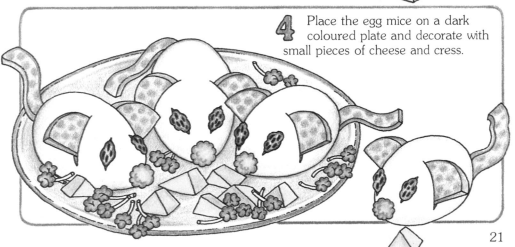

21

Ham Roly-poly Surprise

You will need:

Food:
one 210g can vegetable salad
150g cottage cheese
1 large tomato
salt and pepper
$\frac{1}{2}$ teaspoon tomato ketchup
8 round radishes
8 slices ham
watercress

This makes eight Ham Roly-polys

Equipment:
basin
knife
fork
teaspoon

Before you start, ask a grown-up to open the can of vegetable salad.

1 Spoon the cottage cheese into a basin.

2 Finely chop the tomato and add to the cheese with the salt and pepper and tomato ketchup. Mix well with a fork.

3 Wash the radishes and cut off the tops and tails. Cut each radish in half.

4 Trim any fat off the ham and cut each slice into a large rectangular shape.

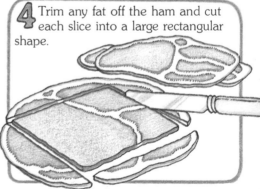

5 Place one of the slices of ham on a flat surface and place a teaspoonful of the cheese and tomato mixture at one corner. Next to this place (along the long edge of the rectangle) a radish half and then a teaspoon of vegetable salad. Put another radish next to this and finish off the row with another spoonful of cheese and tomato.

6 Carefully roll up the ham round the mixed fillings and place on a serving dish.

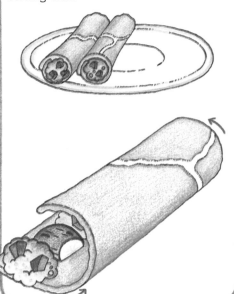

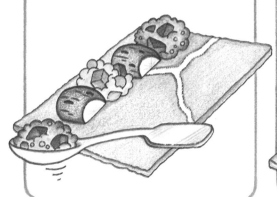

7 Repeat stages five and six for all the pieces of ham. Decorate the plate with sprigs of watercress and serve at once.

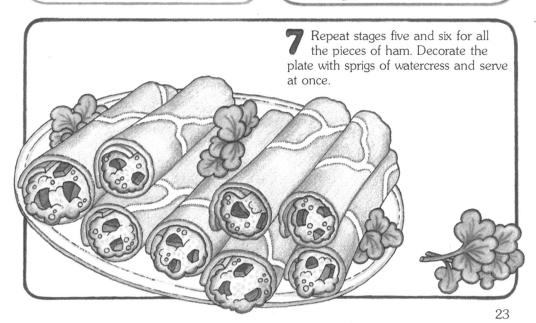

Humpty Dumpty Salad

You will need:

Food:
1 hard boiled egg, shelled
1 slice bread about 2 cm thick
butter
6 cm long piece cucumber
3 raisins
1 slice ham
2 lettuce leaves

This makes one Humpty-Dumpty Salad for one person

Equipment:
knife

Before you start, ask a grown-up to hard boil an egg.

1 Cut the crusts off the slice of bread and spread with butter. Cut in half and then cut each half into three strips to use as building blocks.

2 Cut the cucumber into six slices lengthways and trim each slice to the same size as the bread building blocks.

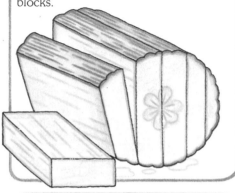

3 Cut a slice off the blunt end of the egg so that it will sit firmly on a flat surface.

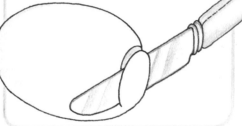

4 Make slits in the egg for eyes, nose and mouth. Press raisins into the slits for eyes and nose and a small strip of ham for the mouth.

5 Place the slice of ham on a plate and arrange two of the bread building blocks in a row with one cucumber block behind them. Make sure that the cucumber block is in the centre.

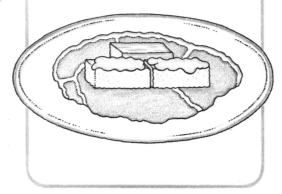

6 Now build up the wall by placing cucumber blocks on top of the bread blocks, and bread blocks on top of the cucumber blocks. Continue in this way until the wall is four rows high.

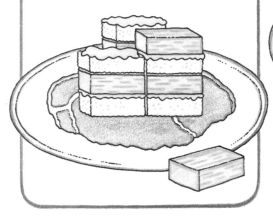

7 Place the Humpty Dumpty egg on the wall.

8 Cut the lettuce leaves into thin strips and spread around the base of the wall to soften Humpty Dumpty's fall!

Family Portrait Biscuits

You will need:

Food:
12 cream crackers or water biscuits
butter
50g of your favourite smooth pâté e.g.
  liver pâté
milk
1 tablespoon mayonnaise
1 teaspoon tomato purée

This makes 12 Family Portrait Biscuits

Equipment:
knife
pieces of greaseproof paper at least
  40cm × 20cm
scissors
tablespoon
teaspoon

1 Spread the biscuits with a little butter and keep on one side.

2 Cut three half circles, each 40cm across the straight edge, out of the greaseproof paper.

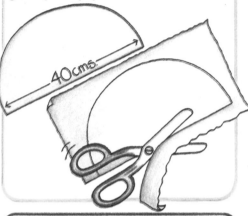

3 Mix the pâté with a little milk until it resembles thick cream.

4 Fold the half circles in half and then in half again. Snip a very small piece off the pointed end of each.

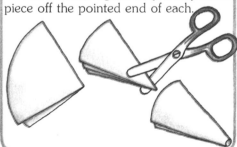

5 Open out the paper to make three cones and fill one with half the pâté mixture. Refill the cone when it's empty.

6 Fill another cone with mayonnaise and the other with tomato purée. Twist the tops of the cones to close them.

7 Pipe out the pâté mixture by squeezing the cone. Use to outline the shape of a head on each biscuit. Fill in the hair with the same mixture, for dark-haired people.

8 Use the mayonnaise for fair-haired members of the family and for cheeks and noses. Use the tomato purée for eyes and mouths.

Caribbean Trifle

You will need:

Food:
one 210g can mandarin oranges
1 Jamaica or ginger cake
1 packet Butterscotch Instant Whip or
  Angel Delight
600ml milk
1 packet milk chocolate buttons

This makes one large Trifle

Equipment:
knife
basin
wire whisk

**Before you start, ask a grown-up to
open the can of oranges.**

2 Pour the contents of the can of oranges over the top. Spread the oranges evenly over the surface of the cake.

3 Using the milk, make up the Instant Whip or Angel Delight as directed on the packet and spoon over the top of the trifle.

1 Slice the Jamaica cake and arrange in the bottom of a glass dish.

4 Decorate with chocolate buttons.

28

Banana Milk Shake

You will need:

Food:
250ml milk
2 teaspoons brown sugar
1 ripe banana

This makes enough for one person

Equipment:
measuring jug
fork and spoon
electric blender or whisk
tall glass

2 Peel and mash the banana and add to the sweetened milk.

1 Measure the milk in a jug and stir in the sugar. Continue stirring until the sugar has all dissolved.

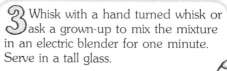

3 Whisk with a hand turned whisk or ask a grown-up to mix the mixture in an electric blender for one minute. Serve in a tall glass.

29

Lime and Lemon Ice Cream Soda

You will need:

Food:
4 scoops vanilla ice cream
4 capfuls concentrated lime juice
600ml fizzy lemonade

This makes four tall glassfuls

Equipment:
ice cream scoop or tablespoon
4 tall glasses
8 straws

1 Place one scoop of ice cream in the bottom of each glass.

2 Carefully measure the capfuls of lime juice and pour one capful over each scoop of ice cream.

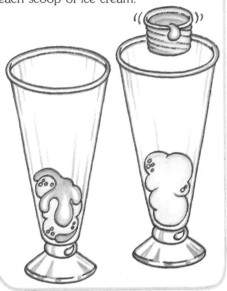

3 Top up with lemonade, sharing it equally between the four glasses. Place two straws in each glass and serve at once.

Striped Lollies

Food:

1 tablespoon blackcurrant squash mixed
 with three tablespoons water
1 tablespoon lime juice mixed with
 three tablespoons water
1 tablespoon orange squash mixed with
 three tablespoons water

This makes four Lollies

Equipment:

tablespoon and 4 egg cups
4 lolly sticks (saved from bought lollies,
 washed and cut to 8 cm in length)

1 Place one tablespoonful of the
blackcurrant mixture in the bottom
of each egg cup. Place one stick in each
cup and put the egg cups in the frozen
food section of the fridge or in the
freezer. Leave for one hour when the
liquid should have frozen solid.

2 Then add one tablespoon of the
lime juice mixture to each egg cup
and return to the freezing compartment
for one hour to freeze.

3 After one hour add the orange
squash mixture and return to the
freezing compartment. The lollies will be
ready to eat after a further hour or so.

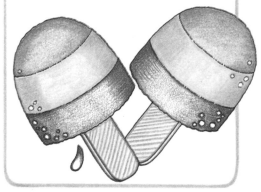

31

No-cook Savouries

Greek Yoghurt Soup

You will need:

Food:
15cm long piece cucumber
2–3 sprigs mint
1 tablespoon raisins
350g plain yoghurt
5 tablespoons milk
salt and pepper
ice cubes

This makes enough for four people

Equipment:
grater
knife
large bowl

2 Finely chop the mint and the raisins and add to the bowl with the cucumber.

3 Pour on the yoghurt and milk and add the salt and pepper. Place in the fridge for an hour to chill.

1 Grate the cucumber into a bowl or cut into very small pieces.

4 Just before serving add some ice cubes to the soup.

33

Tuna Bunwiches

You will need:

Food:
one 150g can tuna fish
1 tablespoon salad cream
salt and pepper
2 hard boiled eggs, shelled
4 teaspoons American relish
4 sesame buns
butter

This makes four buns

Equipment:
small basin
fork
egg slicer
teaspoon
knife

Before you start, ask a grown-up to open the can of tuna fish and hard boil the eggs.

1 Drain the liquid from the open can of tuna and scoop the fish out into a basin. Break up the fish with a fork and mix in the salad cream and salt and pepper.

2 Cut the hard boiled eggs into thin slices.

3 Slice the buns in half and butter each half. Spread the bottom halves with the tuna mixture. Place a few slices of egg on each bun and top with a teaspoonful of relish. Replace the tops of the buns and put the filled Bunwiches on a plate to serve.

Rabbit Biscuits

You will need:

Food:
12 cream crackers
butter
6 slices processed cheese
tube of tomato purée
1 teaspoon mayonnaise
cress

This makes 12 Rabbit Biscuits

Equipment:
knife
teaspoon

1 Butter the cream crackers and put to one side.

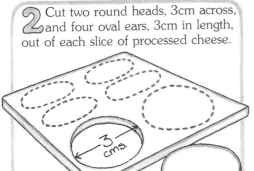

2 Cut two round heads, 3cm across, and four oval ears, 3cm in length, out of each slice of processed cheese.

3 Arrange a head and two ears on each biscuit.

4 Squeeze out blobs of tomato purée for eyes and mouth, and use the mayonnaise for the nose. Finish off by putting cress whiskers in place.

Savoury Pinwheels

You will need:

Food:
225g cream cheese
2–3 tablespoons milk
1 level teaspoon paprika pepper
1 level teaspoon rosemary, thyme,
  tarragon or your favourite herb
6 large slices very fresh bread

This makes about 30 Pinwheels

Equipment:
2 basins
fork
knife

1 Place the cream cheese in one of the basins and mix with 2 tablespoons of milk. If the mixture is still a little too thick to spread smoothly add the rest of the milk.

2 Divide the cream cheese mixture in half and place one portion in the other basin. Mix one lot with paprika and the other with your favourite herb.

3 Cut the crusts off the slices of bread and spread three with the paprika mixture and three with the herb mixture.

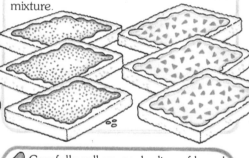

4 Carefully roll up each slice of bread and press the edge down to keep it rolled up. If possible place in a polythene container in the fridge for an hour to chill. Just before serving slice each roll into five pinwheels.

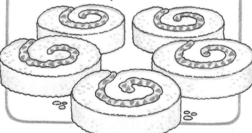

Cheesy Fish

You will need:

Food:
250g cheddar cheese
4cm cucumber
2 tomatoes
75g cream cheese
1 tablespoon salad cream or
  mayonnaise
salt and pepper

This makes enough for one large fish mould

Equipment:
grater
mixing bowl and basin
knife
fork
tablespoon
fish-shaped mould

2 Place the cream cheese in a bowl and mix with the salad cream or mayonnaise to form a smooth cream. Stir it into the cheese and cucumber mixture. Season with salt and pepper.

1 Grate the cheese and cucumber into a mixing bowl. Finely chop the tomatoes and add to the mixture.

3 Spoon the mixture into a fish-shaped mould and chill for two hours. Turn out to serve. You can make other shapes according to the shapes of the moulds you have.

Surprise French Loaf

You will need:

Food:
1 small French loaf (about 40cm in length)
butter
1 small can corned beef
6–8 sprigs watercress
1 teaspoon chutney
1 teaspoon salad cream or mayonnaise
270g can baked beans in tomato sauce
2 tomatoes
6 lettuce leaves

This makes one Surprise Loaf and is enough for four people

Equipment:
knife
tablespoon
2 basins

Before you start, ask a grown-up to open the can of corned beef and the can of beans.

1 Cut the French loaf along its length and scoop out some of the centre dough.

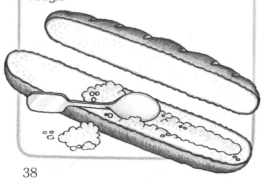

2 Butter the inside of the loaf and put to one side.

3 Chop the corned beef very finely and place in one of the basins.

4 Chop the watercress and add to the corned beef with the chutney and mayonnaise. Mix well together.

5 Spoon the beans into the second basin.

6 Finely chop the tomatoes and add to the beans. Mix well together.

7 Tear the lettuce leaves into smaller pieces and use to line the inside of the French loaf.

8 Spoon alternate mounds of corned beef and watercress, and beans and tomato into the centre of the loaf and replace the top of the loaf. To serve cut into 10cm lengths.

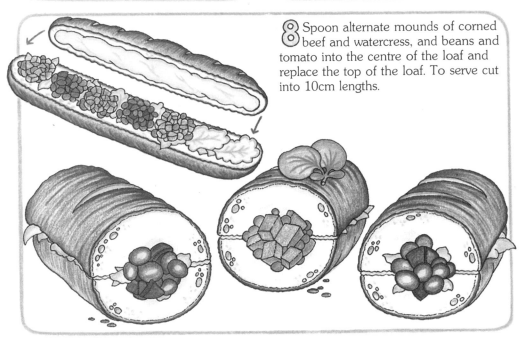

Viking Ship

You will need:

Food:
1 banana
lemon juice
50g hard cheese
3 black and 3 green grapes
1 lettuce leaf
4–5 small radishes

This makes one Viking Ship for one person

Equipment:
scissors
knife
19 cocktail sticks

1 Peel the banana, keeping the peel on one side. Cut a very thin slice off the banana so that it will sit on a flat surface, and coat it with lemon juice to stop it turning brown.

2 Cut the peel off just below the stalk and place the stalk on one end of the banana to form the prow of the boat.

3 Cut the cheese into six small squares and thread each one on to a cocktail stick with one of the grapes.

4 Stick each cocktail stick, cheese end first, upright along the banana. Start with a green grape and then a black grape and so on. These are the Viking crew.

5 Spear the lettuce leaf with another cocktail stick and place towards the front of the boat to make a sail.

6 Cut the radishes into slices. Spear each slice with a cocktail stick to form oars. You will need 12 of them.

7 Stick the oars into the sides of the banana, one by each of the Vikings.

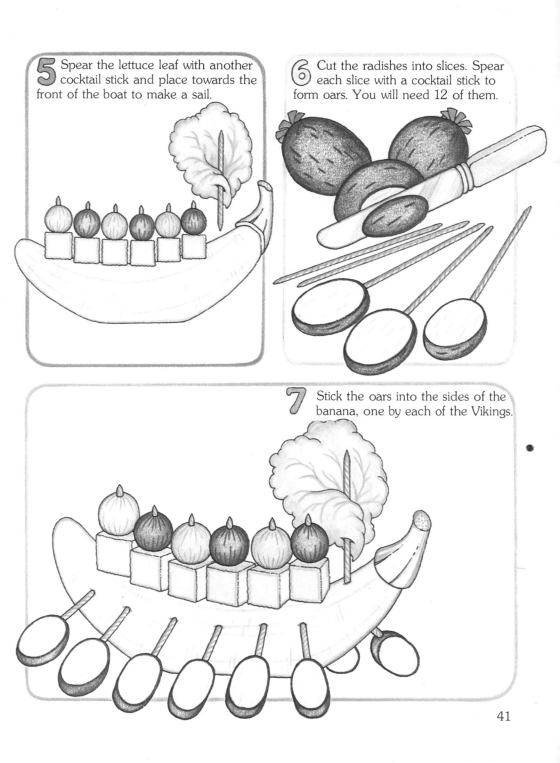

Mimosa Salad

You will need:

Food:
2 hard boiled eggs, shelled
1 small lettuce
sprigs of parsley
4 tablespoons mayonnaise

This makes four Mimosa Salads

Equipment:
knife
sieve
saucer
4 bowls
tablespoon

Before you start, ask a grown-up to hard boil the eggs.

1 When the eggs are cold, cut them in half and separate the yolks from the whites. Very finely chop the whites and put to one side. Press the egg yolks through a sieve and keep on a saucer.

2 Wash the lettuce leaves, drain them, and tear them into small pieces. Very finely chop the parsley.

3 Divide the lettuce between the four bowls and place a tablespoon of mayonnaise on the centre of each bed of lettuce.

4 Sprinkle the chopped egg whites all the way round the outside of the mayonnaise and then sprinkle the sieved egg yolks all over the top. Decorate with chopped parsley. These salads look like the yellow mimosa flowers.

Water Lily Salads

You will need:

Food:
100g black grapes
½ lettuce
1 tablespoon mayonnaise

This makes four Water Lily Salads

Equipment:
knife
tablespoon
teaspoon
4 bowls

1 Halve the grapes and remove the pips.

2 Wash the lettuce and drain well. Arrange pieces of lettuce so that they line the four bowls.

3 Divide the halved grapes into four portions and place a portion in each bowl. Arrange the grapes so that the cut side faces up.

4 Use the tip of the handle of the teaspoon to place small blobs of mayonnaise in the centre of each grape half. These salads look like water lilies with their green leaves.

Bunch of Grapes Salad

You will need:

Food:
150g cream cheese
4 tablespoons sour cream or plain
  yoghurt
salt and pepper
250g black or green grapes
2 ripe pears

This makes four Bunches of Grapes

Equipment:
basin
fork
knife
serving dish

1 Put the cream cheese in the basin with the sour cream or yoghurt and the salt and pepper. Mix well together with a fork.

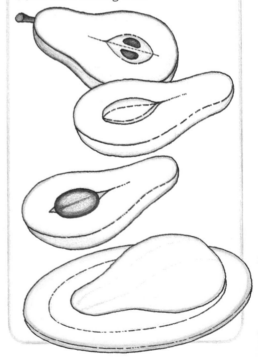

2 Halve the grapes and remove the pips. Keep some of the stalks.

3 Halve and peel the pears and carefully remove the cores. Place a grape half in the hole where the core was and place each half pear cut side down on a serving dish.

44

4 Spread a quarter of the cream cheese mixture over each pear half, following the shape of the pear.

5 Press the halved grapes into the cream cheese in rows going from end to end of the pear. When all the grapes are in place the pear will resemble a bunch of grapes.

6 Finish off by placing a piece of grape stalk at the fatter end. Serve at once or chill in the fridge and serve after an hour.

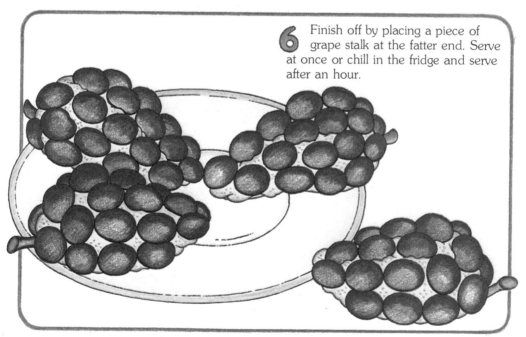

Austrian Salad

You will need:

Food:
4 chipolata or hotdog sausages
100g Austrian smoked cheese
1 green skinned apple
1 red skinned apple
juice of 1 lemon
2 tablespoons salad oil
4 cocktail gherkins
4 sticks celery
2 tomatoes
lettuce leaves

This makes enough for four Austrian Salads

Equipment:
knife
mixing bowl
tablespoon
4 gummed labels
crayons
4 cocktail sticks

1 Very thinly slice the sausage and place in a mixing bowl.

2 Cut the cheese into small cubes and add to the sausages.

3 Quarter the apples and carefully remove the cores. Cut the apples into cubes and place in the mixing bowl.

4 Add the lemon juice and salad oil and mix everything well together.

5 Very finely chop the gherkins and celery and add to the mixture in the bowl.

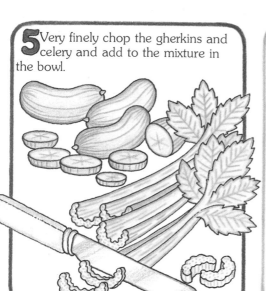

7 Line four bowls with the lettuce and spoon a quarter of the salad mixture into each bowl. Arrange the sliced tomatoes round the outside.

6 Slice the tomatoes and cut each slice in half. Tear the lettuce into smaller pieces.

8 Make four Austrian flags by colouring each label with a band of red at the top and bottom, leaving the centre white. Stick one end of each label round a cocktail stick and stick into the salad.

47

Sunshine Salad

You will need:

Food:
1 hard boiled egg, shelled
1 medium-sized carrot
1 teaspoon salad oil
1 peach half

This makes one Sunshine Salad

Equipment:
sieve
2 saucers
knife
grater
basin

Before you start, ask a grown-up to hard boil an egg.

1 Cut the egg in half. Sieve the yolk on to one saucer and sieve the white on to another.

2 Grate the carrot into a basin. Add the oil and mix well together.

3 Place the peach half in the centre of a small plate and surround with the grated carrot.

4 Sprinkle the sieved egg yolk round the outside of the carrot and the egg white round the outside of the egg yolk. This salad looks like a sun with rays of sunshine.

48

Marigold Heads

You will need:

Food:
1 hard boiled egg, shelled
2 carrots
sprigs of parsley

This makes one Marigold Head

Equipment:
knife and flat plate

Before you start, ask a grown-up to hard boil the egg.

1 Cut the egg in half and separate the yolk from the white. Very finely chop both yolk and white keeping them separate.

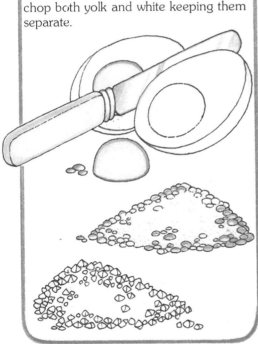

2 Cut the carrots into thin slices along their lengths and shape at least 12 long thin petals out of these slices.

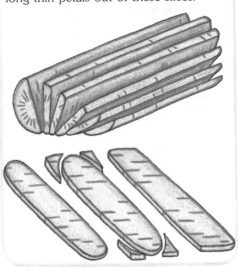

3 Pile the chopped egg yolk in the centre of a flat plate. Arrange the carrot petals round the outside to resemble the petals of a marigold. Use the chopped egg white to make a stalk and decorate with sprigs of parsley as leaves. Serve at once.

Salad Kebabs

You will need:

Food:
3 rashers crispy bacon or 1 thick
  slice ham
2 pineapple rings
$\frac{1}{2}$ green pepper
1 apple
50g hard cheese
12 cocktail onions
lettuce

This makes 12 Kebabs

Equipment:
knife
12 cocktail sticks

Before you start, ask a grown-up to grill the bacon and to open the can of pineapple rings.

1 Cut each cooked rasher of bacon into six pieces or cut the ham into 18 small pieces.

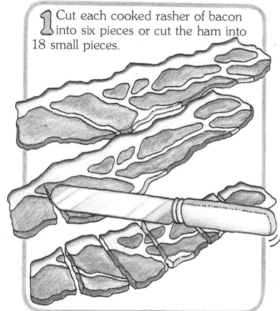

2 Cut each pineapple ring into six pieces.

3 Remove the seeds from the green pepper and cut the green part into 12 pieces.

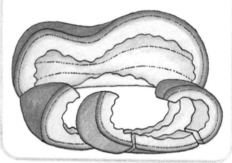

4 Cut the apple into halves and remove the core. Cut into 12 pieces.

50

5 Cut the cheese into 12 cubes and line up all the ingredients on the work surface.

7 Thread the remaining six cocktail sticks as follows: one piece of apple, one piece of cheese, one cocktail onion, one piece of apple, one piece of cheese, one cocktail onion.

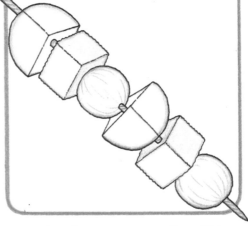

6 Thread six of the cocktail sticks as follows: one piece of pineapple, one piece of bacon or ham, one piece of green pepper, one piece of bacon or ham, one piece of pineapple, one piece of bacon or ham, one piece of green pepper.

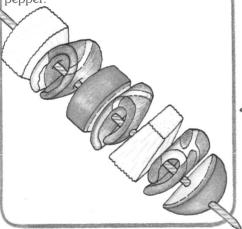

8 Arrange the lettuce on a serving plate and place the kebabs on the top.

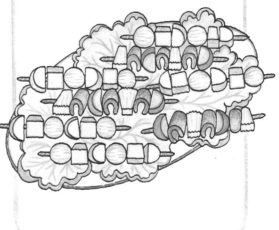

Stuffed Eggs

You will need:

Food:
4 hard boiled eggs, shelled
6 teaspoons mayonnaise
2–3 sprigs parsley
$\frac{1}{2}$ level teaspoon curry powder
4–5 sprigs watercress

This makes eight Stuffed Egg halves

Equipment:
knife
fork
teaspoon
2 basins

Before you start, ask a grown-up to hard boil the eggs. Leave them to cool.

1 Cut the eggs in half. Take out the egg yolks and place them in one of the basins. Place the egg whites on a serving plate.

2 Mash the egg yolks with a fork and add the mayonnaise. Divide the mixture between the two basins.

3 Very finely chop the parsley and mix with one of the portions of egg yolk. Mix the curry powder with the other portion.

4 Place teaspoonfuls of the parsley mixture in four of the egg whites, and teaspoonfuls of the curried mixture in the remaining four. Decorate with sprigs of watercress.

52

Teatime Treats

Coconut Mountains

You will need:

Food:
225g desiccated coconut
387g can condensed milk

This makes 12–14 Mountains

Equipment:
mixing bowl
dessertspoon
baking tray

Before you start, ask a grown-up to set the oven to 120°C/325°F/Gas 3 and open the can of condensed milk.

2 Place the desiccated coconut and the condensed milk in the mixing bowl. Mix well together with the spoon.

1 Grease the baking tray with a little oil or margarine and sprinkle with flour. Shake the tray to spread the flour. Shake off any that remains free.

3 Place spoonfuls of the mixture on the baking tray, leaving the dollops jagged like a rocky mountain. Ask a grown-up to bake the mountains for 30 minutes until the peaks are golden in colour, and to take them out of the oven for you. Use a fish slice to transfer the mountains to a wire rack to cool.

54

American Muffins

You will need:

Food:
25g butter
200g wholemeal flour
1 level teaspoon sugar
$\frac{1}{2}$ level teaspoon salt
2 level teaspoons baking powder
1 egg
150ml milk

This makes nine Muffins

Equipment:
mixing bowl
basin
fork
dessertspoon
non-stick bun tray

Before you start ask a grown-up to melt the butter and to set the oven to 220°C/425°F/Gas 7.

2 Break the egg into a basin and mix well with a fork. Add the milk and melted butter.

3 Pour the egg mixture over the dry ingredients and beat well together.

1 Place the flour, sugar, salt and baking powder in the mixing bowl.

4 Place dessertspoonfuls of the mixture in each hollow in the bun tray. Ask a grown-up to bake the muffins in the oven for 15–20 minutes. Eat with butter.

Banana Tea Bread

You will need:

Food:
75g butter or margarine
125g sugar
1 large egg
3 large ripe bananas
25g walnuts
25g raisins
225g plain flour
½ teaspoon salt
2 teaspoons baking powder
1–2 tablespoons milk

This makes one loaf

Equipment:
mixing bowl
wooden spoon
fork and plate
knife
sieve
tablespoon
750g non-stick loaf tin

Before you start, ask a grown-up to set the oven to 180°C/350°F/Gas 4.

2 Add the sugar and egg and beat again for two minutes.

3 Peel the bananas and place on a plate. Mash well with a fork until the bananas are smooth and creamy.

4 Finely chop the walnuts.

1 Place the butter in the mixing bowl and beat with a wooden spoon until it is smooth <u>and creamy</u>.

5 Mix the creamed bananas into the butter, sugar and egg mixture and then stir in the nuts and raisins.

7 Spoon the mixture into the loaf tin and ask a grown-up to bake it in the oven for $1\frac{1}{4}$–$1\frac{1}{2}$ hours until golden brown on top.

6 Next sift the flour and add to the mixing bowl with the salt and baking powder. Fold the mixture together with a tablespoon. If the mixture is too stiff to drop easily off the spoon add a little milk.

8 Ask a grown-up to test the bread to see if it is done by running a skewer through the centre. If it comes out clean the bread is cooked.

Herb Bread

You will need:

Food:
3–4 sprigs parsley
50g butter
1 level teaspoon dried mixed herbs
1 medium length French loaf

This is enough for one loaf

Equipment:
knife
basin
wooden spoon
aluminium foil

Before you start, ask a grown-up to set the oven to 240°C/450°F/Gas 6.

1 Finely chop the parsley. Tip into a basin and mix with the butter and mixed herbs. Continue mixing until a smooth paste is formed.

2 Start to cut the French loaf into slices but don't cut right through to the bottom.

3 Spread each slice with the herb butter.

4 Wrap up the loaf in aluminium foil and ask a grown-up to bake it in the oven for 6–8 minutes until crisp and golden.

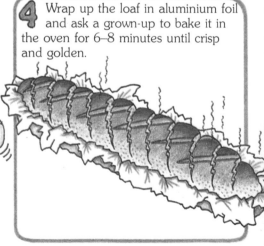

Johnny Bread

You will need:

Food:
150g polenta or yellow cornmeal
75g plain flour
1 level teaspoon salt
2 level teaspoons baking powder
1 egg
200ml milk
2 tablespoons honey
3 tablespoons corn oil

This makes one loaf of Johnny Bread

Equipment:
mixing bowl
teaspoon
basin
fork
tablespoon
20cm × 20cm baking tin

Before you start, ask a grown-up to set the oven to 190°C/375°F/Gas 5. Grease the baking tin with a little oil or margarine.

1 Place the cornmeal, flour, salt and baking powder in the mixing bowl and mix well together.

2 Break the egg into the basin and beat with a fork. Add the milk and honey and beat until the honey is dissolved into the mixture. Add the oil.

3 Pour the liquid mixture over the cornmeal and flour mixture. Stir well and pour into the baking tin. Ask a grown-up to bake it in the oven for about one hour until firm in the centre. Eat hot with butter.

59

Biscuit Cake

You will need:

Food:
juice of 1 large orange
125ml double cream
1 tablespoon sugar
a few drops of vanilla essence
1 packet of your favourite kind of sweet
  biscuit
orange and lemon jellied slices

This makes one Cake

Equipment:
soup bowl or shallow dish
basin
fork or wire whisk
knife
lemon squeezer
plate

1 Squeeze the orange using the lemon squeezer and put the juice in the soup bowl.

2 Pour the cream into the basin. Add the sugar and vanilla essence and beat with a fork or wire whisk until fairly stiff.

3 Dip one biscuit into the orange juice. Count to four and turn it over. Count to four again and lift it out, shaking off any juice.

4 Spread the biscuit with a little cream and put it on a plate.

5 Dip all the remaining biscuits in the orange and spread with cream. Place each one on top of the other.

7 When all the biscuits have been sandwiched together, cover the roll with the remaining cream.

6 After you have dipped and creamed five or six biscuits you will be able to turn the biscuits on their sides and build up a long roll.

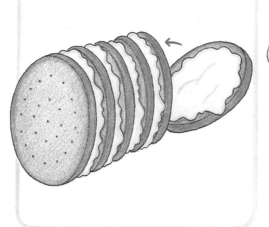

8 Decorate with the orange and lemon slices and place in the fridge to chill for two hours. Serve by cutting diagonally with a knife.

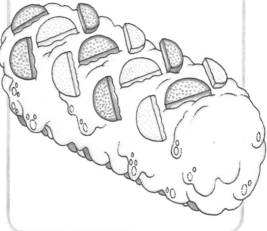

Initial Biscuits

You will need:

Food:
icing sugar
50g almond marzipan
6–8 level teaspoons raspberry jam
6–8 digestive biscuits

This makes about 6–8 Initial Biscuits

Equipment:
rolling pin
knife
teaspoon

2 Cut the marzipan in half and cut three initials (from your friends' or your family's names) out of each half. Press the trimmings together and roll out again. Use to make one or two more letters.

1 Sprinkle your work surface with a little icing sugar and roll out the marzipan to a rectangle 12cm × 14cm.

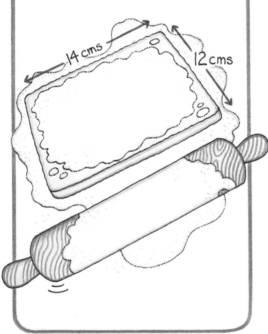

14 cms

12 cms

3 Spread each biscuit with a level teaspoonful of jam and press one marzipan initial on top of each biscuit.

Rock Buns

You will need:

Food:
200g self-raising flour
pinch salt
75g butter or margarine
75g sugar
50g raisins
25g chopped candied peel
1 egg
1–2 tablespoons milk

This makes about 10–12 Rock Buns

Equipment:
mixing bowl
sieve
basin
knife and fork
dessertspoon
non-stick baking tray

Before you start ask a grown-up to set the oven to 180°C/350°F/Gas 4.

2 Mix in the sugar, raisins and candied peel.

3 Break the egg into a basin and beat with one tablespoon of milk. Pour over the 'breadcrumb' mixture and mix with a fork. If the mixture is very stiff add a little more milk.

1 Sift the flour and salt into the mixing bowl. Cut the butter or margarine into small pieces and add to the flour. Rub the butter into the flour, using the tips of your fingers, until the mixture resembles fine breadcrumbs.

4 Place heaped dessertspoons of the mixture on the baking tray leaving plenty of space between each one. Leave the heaps jagged to give a rocky effect. Ask a grown-up to bake the buns in the oven for about 10–15 minutes until they are golden brown and firm.

63

Artist's Cake

You will need:

Food:
1 sponge cake
225g icing sugar and 2 tablespoons hot
  water; or packet of icing fondant
  and some jam
red, yellow, blue and green food colours
a little water

This makes one Artist's Cake

Equipment:
sieve, bowl and spoon
rolling pin
board
palette knife and knife
piece of paper and crayons
paint brush

1 Sieve the icing sugar into a bowl and mix with the hot water to form a smooth paste (glacé icing), or roll out the fondant icing.

2 Place the cake on a board and spread the glacé icing all over it. Or spread the cake with jam and cut the fondant icing to fit the cake and press into place.

3 Leave to dry for two hours and plan your picture on paper.

4 Draw an outline of your picture on the cake, using the dip sticks of the food colours.

5 Fill in with food colour, or for a lighter effect mix the food colours with a little water and brush on with a clean paint brush.

6 Leave to dry and serve to the art critics!

65

Shortbread Alphabet

You will need:

Food:
150g plain flour
75g sugar
pinch salt
100g butter

This makes about 10 letters of the alphabet

Equipment:
mixing bowl
knife
rolling pin
non-stick baking tray

Before you start, ask a grown-up to set the oven to 180°C/350°F/Gas 4.

1 Place the flour, sugar and salt in the mixing bowl. Cut the butter into small pieces and add to the bowl.

2 Rub the butter into the flour and sugar mixture using the tips of your fingers. When the butter and flour begin to form crumbs start to knead the mixture by pressing down with your knuckles.

3 Press this dough into a firm lump. Sprinkle flour on your work surface and place the dough on it. Roll it out until it is about 1cm thick.

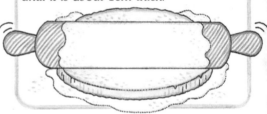

4 Using a knife, cut out shapes of the alphabet making sure that the strips making the letters are at least 1½cm wide. Place the letters on the baking tray. Use the trimmings to make another two letters. Ask a grown-up to bake the letters in the oven for about 20 minutes until golden in colour. Leave them to cool on the tray.

Soda Bread

You will need:

Food:
225g wholemeal flour
3 level teaspoons baking powder
1 level teaspoon brown sugar
1 level teaspoon salt
300ml milk

This makes one loaf

Equipment:
mixing bowl
wooden spoon
non-stick baking tray
knife

Before you start, ask a grown-up to set the oven to 190°C/375°F/Gas 5.

2 Make a well in the centre and pour in the milk. Mix together all the ingredients with the spoon.

1 Place the flour, baking powder, sugar and salt in a bowl.

3 Flour your hands and shape the dough into a ball. Place on the baking tray. Mark the top of the loaf into four quarters with a knife, cutting about halfway through the dough. Ask a grown-up to bake it in the oven for 30 minutes.

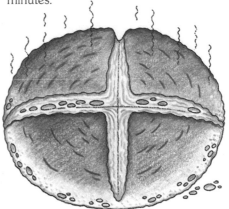

This bread is best eaten on the same day as it is made.

St. Nicholas Biscuits

You will need:

Food:
100g flour
25g brown sugar
1 level teaspoon baking powder
pinch of salt
1 level teaspoon cinnamon
$\frac{1}{4}$ level teaspoon nutmeg
$\frac{1}{4}$ level teaspoon allspice
50g butter or margarine
2 tablespoons milk
1 tablespoon flaked almonds

This makes enough for eight Biscuits

Equipment:
mixing bowl
knife
tablespoon
fish slice
non-stick baking tray
pastry brush

Before you start, ask a grown-up to set the oven to 180°C/350°F/Gas 4.

1 Place the flour, sugar, baking powder, salt and spices in the mixing bowl. Cut the butter or margarine into small pieces and add to the bowl.

2 Rub the butter into the spiced flour and sugar mixture using the tips of your fingers. Continue rubbing in until the mixture resembles fine breadcrumbs.

3 Add one tablespoon of the milk. Knead the mixture with your knuckles and press into a firm lump.

4 Sprinkle flour on the work surface and place the lump of dough on this. Press out with your hand to form a circle about 16cm across. Use a fish slice to move the circle from the work surface to the baking tray.

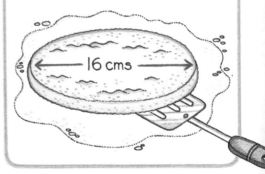

16 cms

5 Brush the top of the circle with a little milk and sprinkle the flaked almonds over the top. Press the almonds into the surface of the circle.

6 Ask a grown-up to bake the circle in the oven for 25 minutes.

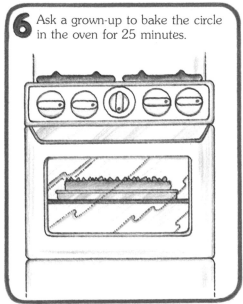

7 When the circle is cooked, cut it into four quarters and then cut each quarter into two to make eight pieces. Use a fish slice to place on a wire rack to cool.

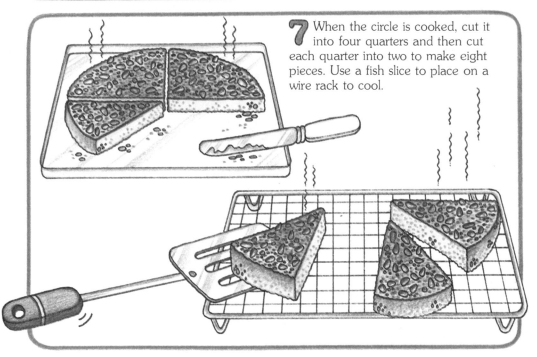

Chocolate Butterfly Cakes

You will need:

Food:
(for the cakes)
100g butter or margarine
100g castor sugar
2 eggs
100g self-raising flour
1 tablespoon cocoa powder
1 level teaspoon baking powder

(for the icing)
1 teaspoon cocoa powder
2 teaspoons hot water
250g icing sugar
125g butter

Equipment:
mixing bowl and sieve
wooden spoon
tablespoon and teaspoon
knife
basin
non-stick bun tray

Before you start ask a grown-up to set the oven to 200°C/400°F/Gas 6.

1 Place the butter or margarine, sugar, and eggs in the mixing bowl.

2 Sift the flour, cocoa powder and baking powder over the top.

3 Beat all these together for about 2–3 minutes with a wooden spoon until smooth.

4 Spoon the mixture into the bun tray. Ask a grown-up to bake the buns in the oven for about 10–12 minutes until they are well risen and firm to the touch.

5 While the buns are cooking make the icing. Mix the cocoa with the hot water in the basin and stir until the cocoa powder has dissolved.

6 Add the butter and sugar to the basin and mix until really smooth and creamy.

7 Ask a grown-up to remove the buns from the oven and place them on a wire rack to cool. When they are cold cut straight across the buns, removing the tops. Cut these tops into two to form the butterfly wings.

8 Spoon a little of the butter icing on to each bun and stick the two wings into the icing at an angle to each other.

Hot Cross Buns

You will need:

Food:
500g plain flour
150ml lukewarm milk
150ml lukewarm water
1 level teaspoon sugar
1 level tablespoon dried yeast
$\frac{1}{2}$ level teaspoon ground cinnamon
$\frac{1}{2}$ level teaspoon ground nutmeg
$\frac{1}{2}$ level teaspoon ground mixed spices
50g sugar
100g raisins
50g chopped candied peel
50g butter
2 eggs
1 tablespoon milk

This makes 12 Hot Cross Buns

Equipment:
sieve and basin
teaspoon
tablespoon
mixing bowl
fork
non-stick baking tray
polythene sheet, greased
pastry brush

1 Sift 100g of the flour into the basin with the milk and mix to a smooth cream. Add the sugar and water. Sprinkle the yeast over the top and leave to stand for 20 minutes.

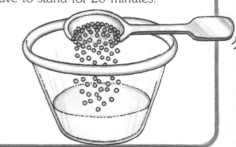

2 Sift the rest of the flour into the mixing bowl. Add the spices, sugar, raisins and candied peel.

3 Ask a grown-up to melt the butter and mix this into the yeast mixture which should now be frothy. Add one of the eggs and beat the mixture with a fork.

4 Pour the liquid ingredients over the bowl of dry ingredients and mix to a smooth dough, starting off with a spoon and finishing off with your fingers.

5 Sprinkle the work surface with a little flour and place the ball of dough on this. Knead the dough for 10 minutes until it is really smooth and elastic.

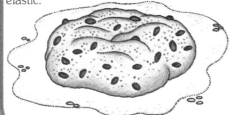

6 Divide the dough into 12 equal portions. Shape into buns, turning the edges to the middle to make the under sides flat.

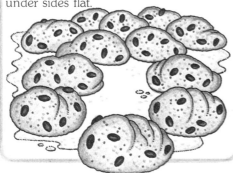

7 Place, well spread out, on the baking tray. Cover with a greased polythene sheet and leave in a warm place to rise.

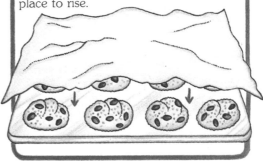

8 Ask a grown-up to set the oven to 220°C/425°F/Gas 7. Cut a cross in the top of each bun.

9 Beat the remaining egg with a little milk and use to brush all over the top of the buns. Ask a grown-up to bake the buns in the oven for about 20 minutes until golden brown in colour.

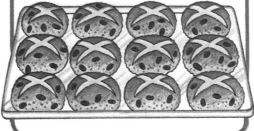

73

Gingerbread Catherine Wheels

You will need:

Food:
50g butter or margarine
25g brown sugar
1 heaped tablespoon black treacle
1 level teaspoon ground ginger
pinch of salt
100g self-raising flour
10 hazelnuts or large raisins

This makes about 10 Wheels

Equipment:
mixing bowl
tablespoon
teaspoon
wooden spoon
fish slice
non-stick baking tray

Before you start ask a grown-up to set the oven to 180°C/350°F/Gas 4.

1 Place the butter and sugar in the mixing bowl and mix together with a wooden spoon. Continue mixing until the mixture is light and creamy. Add the treacle and beat this in with the wooden spoon.

2 Add the ground ginger, salt and flour. Start by stirring with a tablespoon and then use your hands to knead the mixture together.

3 When the flour is thoroughly mixed in, sprinkle the work surface with flour.

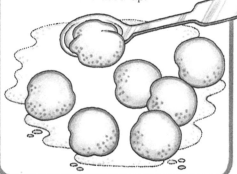

4 Take a teaspoonful of the biscuit mixture and roll it into a ball in your hands. Continue making balls until all the mixture is used up.

5 Next roll the balls into long snakes about 36cm in length.

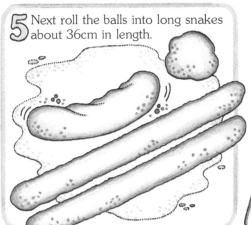

6 Bend round the end of each snake and continue to wind the rest of the snake round to form a Catherine Wheel. Place the wound Catherine Wheel on the baking tray and wind up the rest of the snakes and place them on the tray.

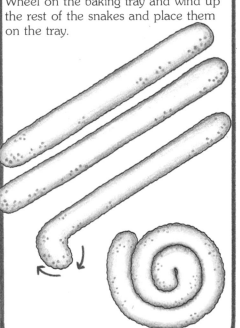

7 Push a hazelnut or large raisin into the centre of each Catherine Wheel. Ask a grown-up to bake the Catherine Wheels on the top shelf of the oven for 15 minutes.

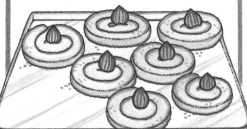

8 When they are cooked, leave them on the tray to cool for a minute or two and then, using a fish slice, transfer them to a wire rack to cool completely.

Hot Meals and Snacks

Cheese, Onion and Potato Pie

You will need:

Food:
600g potatoes
2 onions
100g cheese
250ml milk
salt and pepper

This makes a Pie large enough for four people

Equipment:
knife
grater
large pie dish
baking tray

Before you start, ask a grown-up to set the oven to 190°C/375°F/Gas 5.

1 Peel and slice the onions and potatoes and grate the cheese.

2 Place a layer of potato in the bottom of the pie dish and cover with a layer of onions and then a layer of cheese. Sprinkle with salt and pepper.

3 Repeat the layers and pour on the milk. Ask a grown-up to place the pie dish on a baking tray and to bake in the oven for one hour.

Creamy Spinach Crunch

You will need:

Food:
*286g can condensed cream of chicken
soup
500g frozen leaf spinach
25g cheese
1 packet potato crisps*

**This makes enough for four people to
have with hamburgers or sausages**

Equipment:
*sieve
basin
grater
fork
casserole dish*

**Before you start, ask a grown-up to
open the can of soup and to set the
oven to 200°C/400°F/Gas 6. Thaw
the spinach and drain in a sieve.**

1 Squeeze all the liquid out of the
spinach and place in a basin. Add
the soup and half a canful of water. Mix
well with a fork.

2 Spoon the mixture into a casserole
dish.

3 Grate the cheese and crush the
potato crisps and sprinkle both of
them over the spinach mixture. Ask a
grown-up to bake the dish in the oven
for 20 minutes.

Porcupine Stew

You will need:

Food:
1 onion
400g minced beef
1 egg
100g uncooked long grain rice
salt and pepper
286g can condensed tomato or
  vegetable soup

**This makes 12 Porcupines and is
enough for four people**

Equipment:
knife
2 basins
fork
soup bowl or shallow dish
casserole dish with lid

*Before you start ask a grown-up to
open the can of soup and to set the
oven to 190°C/375°F/Gas 5.*

1 Finely chop the onion and place in
one of the basins with the minced
beef, egg, 50g of rice and salt and
pepper. Mix very well with a fork.

2 Empty the soup into another basin
and add a canful of water. Mix with
a fork.

3 Shape the minced beef mixture into
12 small balls. Place the rest of the
rice in a soup bowl and roll the balls in
the rice before placing in the casserole
dish.

4 Pour the soup over the top. Cover
and ask a grown-up to cook the
stew in the oven for 45 minutes.

79

Salmon Owls

You will need:

Food:
200g can salmon
4 spring onions or $\frac{1}{2}$ small onion
sprigs of parsley
200g cream cheese
100g stale bread
salt and pepper
1 egg
1 carrot

This makes eight Salmon Owls

Equipment:
basin
fork
knife
2 soup bowls or shallow dishes
non-stick baking tray

Before you start ask a grown-up to set the oven to 200°C/400°F/Gas 6 and to open the can of salmon.

1 Drain any liquid off the salmon and then place the salmon in the basin. Break up and mash with a fork.

2 Very finely chop the spring onions or onion and the parsley. Add to the salmon with the cream cheese, salt and pepper and mix well together.

3 Make breadcrumbs with the stale bread by rubbing the bread between your hands. Breadcrumbs can also be made by grating the bread.

4 Mix half the breadcrumbs into the salmon and cream cheese mixture and place the other half in a soup bowl.

5 Break the egg into the other soup bowl and beat with a fork.

6 Shape the salmon and cheese mixture into eight owl shapes or ovals.

7 Dip each one first in the beaten egg and then in the breadcrumbs. Make sure that they are each well covered with breadcrumbs. Put the owls on the baking tray.

8 Peel and slice the carrot. Cut the slices into small triangular pieces to make eyes and beaks. Press these pieces into the owls to make faces. Ask a grown-up to bake the owls in the oven for 15 minutes.

Melting Moments

You will need:

Food:
4 slices processed cheese
4 slices bread
butter
2 teaspoons tomato ketchup

This makes enough for four Melting Moments

Equipment:
knife
teaspoon

Before you start ask a grown-up to heat the grill.

1 Cut picture shapes out of the slices of cheese. Try an aeroplane, a flower with petals, a cat and a motor car.

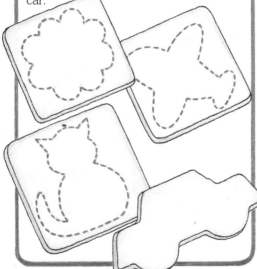

2 Place the slices of bread on the grill pan and toast one side. Be very careful when you are using the grill – you may need help from a grown-up, especially if the grill is high up.

3 Butter the other side of the bread and spread each slice with half a teaspoonful of tomato ketchup.

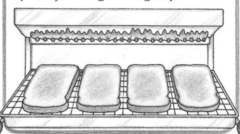

4 Place one picture shape on the buttered side of each piece of toast and place under the grill for a minute or two until the cheese starts to melt.

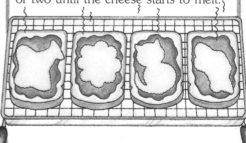

Sausage Cannon

Food:
8 cooked pork or beef sausages or
  hotdog sausages
8 thin slices bread
2 tablespoons tomato ketchup
4 rashers streaky bacon
15g butter

This makes eight Sausage Cannon

Equipment:
knife
non-stick baking tray
8 cocktail sticks

**Before you start ask a grown-up to
cook the sausages or to open the can
of hot dogs and to set the oven to
200°C/400°F/Gas 6.**

1 Cut the crusts off the slices of
bread and lightly butter one side.
Spread the other side with tomato
ketchup.

2 Place a sausage on the tomato side
of the piece of bread and roll up
like a swiss roll.

3 Cut the rind off the streaky bacon
and stretch out the rasher by
running the blade of the knife flat along
the bacon. Cut each stretched rasher
in half.

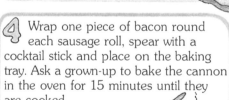

4 Wrap one piece of bacon round
each sausage roll, spear with a
cocktail stick and place on the baking
tray. Ask a grown-up to bake the cannon
in the oven for 15 minutes until they
are cooked.

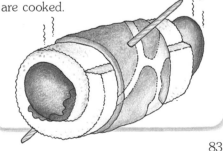

Burgermasters' Council

You will need:

Food:
4–8 beefburgers
4 sesame buns, cut in half
4 lettuce leaves
4 slices processed cheese
8 dried apricot halves
8 raisins
1 radish
1 tomato
2 cocktail gherkins

This makes four Burgermasters

Equipment:
knife

Before you start ask a grown-up to cook the beefburgers.

1 While the beefburgers are being cooked, line up all the ingredients on the work surface.

2 Cut the radish into quarters.

3 Slice the tomato into four slices. Discard the rounded ends. Cut out the centre of each slice, leaving rings of tomato. Cut each ring in two.

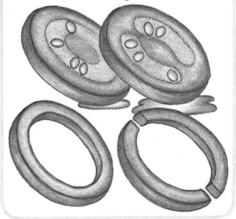

4 Cut the gherkins in half lengthways.

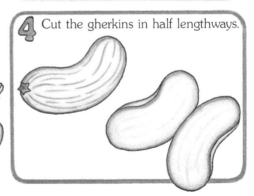

84

5 When the beefburgers are cooked, place the top half of the sesame buns with the seed side down on a large serving plate.

6 On each bun half put a leaf of lettuce, then a cooked beefburger, a slice of cheese and a second beefburger if you are feeling hungry. Cover with the base of the bun.

7 Make faces on each bun base using the apricot halves with a raisin in the centre for eyes, quarter radishes for noses and half gherkins for mouths. Finish off by placing the curved pieces of tomatoes in place as eyebrows. Serve at once.

Fisherman's Parcels

You will need:

Food:
4 cod steaks
4 tomatoes
4 spring onions or $\frac{1}{2}$ small onion
1 teaspoon mixed herbs
4 teaspoons cooking oil

This makes four Fisherman's Parcels

Equipment:
aluminium foil
pair of scissors
knife
teaspoon
baking tray

Before you start ask a grown-up to set the oven to 180°C/350°F/Gas 4.

1 Cut the foil into four pieces about 25cm × 14cm.

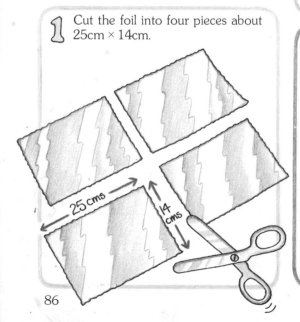

2 Place a cod steak in the centre of each piece of foil.

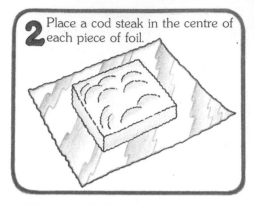

3 Slice the tomatoes and the spring onions or onion and arrange on top of the four fish. Sprinkle each one with herbs and a teaspoon of oil.

4 Wrap up each piece of fish like a parcel, making sure that there are no holes for the steam to escape. Place the parcels on a baking tray and ask a grown-up to cook the fish in the oven for 20 minutes.

Be careful when you open the parcels as the steam will rush out.

Potato Celeste

You will need:

Food:
500g cooked potatoes
4 hard boiled eggs, shelled
one 298g can condensed mushroom
 soup
100g button mushrooms
4 tablespoons milk

This makes enough for four people

Equipment:
knife
basin
tablespoon
1 litre casserole dish with a lid

**Before you start, ask a grown-up to
cook the potatoes, hard boil the
eggs, open the can of soup, and set
the oven to 190°C/375°F/Gas 5.**

1 Slice the cooked potatoes, boiled
eggs and mushrooms and keep
them in separate piles.

2 Spoon the soup into a basin and
mix with the milk to form a fairly
smooth cream.

3 Place a layer of sliced potato in the
bottom of the casserole dish. Cover
this with a layer of sliced egg and then
sliced mushrooms. Pour on half the
mushroom soup. Repeat these layers
again. Cover with a lid and ask a
grown-up to bake the dish in the oven
for 45 minutes.

87

Savoury Drumsticks

You will need:

Food:
8 chicken drumsticks
8 rashers streaky bacon (smoked or
   unsmoked)
6 level tablespoons Parsley and Thyme
   Stuffing Mix
salt and pepper
1 egg

This makes enough for four people

Equipment:
knife
tablespoon
2 soup bowls or shallow dishes
basin
fork
non-stick baking tray

Before starting ask a grown-up to skin the drumsticks and to set the oven to 190°C/375°F/Gas Mark 5.

1 Cut the rind off the bacon and wrap one rasher round each drumstick. Start at the thin end and spiral up towards the fatter end of the drumstick.

2 Spoon the dry stuffing mix into one soup bowl. Break the egg into the basin, add salt and pepper and beat well with a fork. Pour the beaten egg into the other soup bowl.

3 Dip each bacon-wrapped drumstick in the beaten egg and then roll in the stuffing mix. Make sure that each drumstick is well covered and that there are no bare patches. Place the coated drumsticks on the baking tray. Ask a grown-up to cook the drumsticks in the oven for one hour. Serve hot or cold.

Ploughman's Savoury Pudding

You will need:

Food:
5 slices bread
butter
1 onion
100g cheese
2 eggs
500ml milk
salt and pepper

This makes enough for four people

Equipment:
knife
grater
basin
litre pie dish

Before you start ask a grown-up to set the oven to 180°C/350°F/Gas 4.

1 Butter the slices of bread and cut into quarters. Grease the pie dish.

2 Finely slice the onion and grate the cheese.

3 Break the eggs into a basin, add the milk and salt and pepper and beat well.

4 Layer the bread, onion and cheese in the pie dish starting and ending with a layer of bread. Pour on the egg and milk mixture and leave to stand for ½ hour. Ask a grown-up to bake the pudding in the oven for about one hour until it is golden brown in colour and set in the middle.

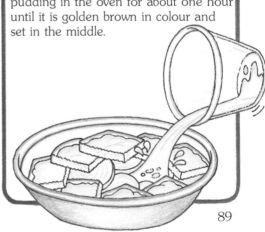

89

Corn Dog Stew

You will need:

Food:
400g can hot dog sausages
396g can tomatoes
198g can sweetcorn
1 onion
salt and pepper
2 packets bacon Frazzles

This makes enough Stew for four people

Equipment:
knife
tablespoon
saucepan with a lid
soup bowl or shallow dish

Before you start ask a grown-up to open the cans.

2 Add the contents of the can of tomatoes. Break up the tomatoes with a spoon.

1 Drain the hot dogs and cut into chunks about 2cm long. Put in the saucepan.

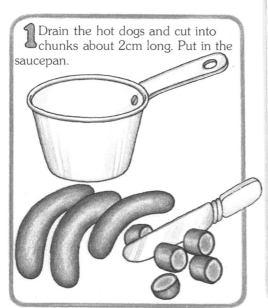

3 Drain the sweetcorn and add to the pan.

90

4 Finely chop the onion and add to the other ingredients with the salt and pepper.

5 Ask a grown-up to bring the stew to the boil and cook in the saucepan for 30 minutes, simmering gently.

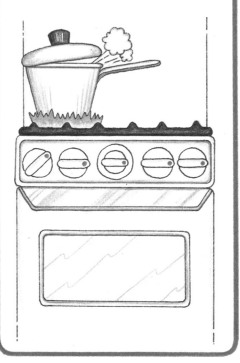

6 Crush the Frazzles between your fingers and keep in a bowl.

7 When the stew is cooked ask a grown-up to spoon it into a shallow serving dish. Sprinkle the top of the dish with the crushed Frazzles.

Canadian Pasties

You will need:

Food:
small packet (215g) frozen puff pastry
140g can condensed mushroom soup
1 hard boiled egg
8 skinless pork sausages
2 teaspoons tomato ketchup
salt and pepper
flour
milk

This makes six Pasties

Equipment:
knife
basin
fork
rolling pin
saucer
tablespoon
non-stick baking tray
pastry brush

Before you start ask a grown-up to hard boil the egg, open the can of soup and set the oven to 200°C/400°F/Gas 6. Thaw the pastry.

1 Shell the egg and chop finely. Place in the basin.

2 Cut the sausages in half lengthways and then cut into small pieces. Add to the basin with the egg.

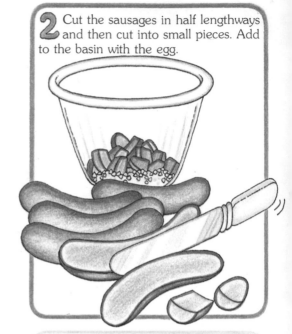

3 Stir in the soup, tomato ketchup and salt and pepper and mix everything well together.

4 Sprinkle a little flour on the working surface and roll out the pastry to make a large square about 30cm × 30cm. Cut out four circles by cutting round the outside of a saucer with a knife. Place the circles to one side.

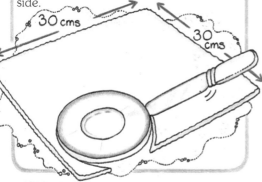

5 Push the pastry trimmings together and roll out again. Cut two further circles from the pastry.

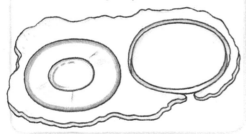

6 Divide the sausage and egg mixture into six portions and place one portion on each circle of pastry.

7 Brush the edge of each circle with water and fold one side over to the other. Pinch together with your fingers so that the pastry sticks together. This also makes an attractive pattern.

8 Place the pasties on the baking tray. Brush the tops with a little milk. Ask a grown-up to bake the pasties in the oven for about 45 minutes until the pastry is golden brown in colour.

Noughts and Crosses Pizza

You will need:

Food:
1 ready-made pizza base or a thick slice of
  bread cut along the length of a loaf
1 tablespoon pizza sauce or tomato
  purée
25g cheese
1 slice cooked ham
1 small tomato
$\frac{1}{4}$ green pepper or 4 anchovy fillets

**This makes one Noughts and Crosses
Pizza for one person**

Equipment:
grater
knife

**Before you start ask a grown-up to
heat the grill. Be careful using the
grill and if it is high up, ask a grown-
up for help.**

1 If you are using bread, lightly toast
it on both sides until just golden in
colour.

2 Place the pizza base or toasted
bread in the grill pan and spread
the pizza sauce or tomato purée all
over the top.

3 Grate the cheese and sprinkle all
over the pizza.

4 Cut the ham into long thin strips about 1cm wide. Arrange the strips on top of the cheese in a criss-cross pattern such as you would draw to play noughts and crosses.

6 Cut the green pepper into thin strips or cut the anchovies in half. Arrange in crosses on the empty squares.

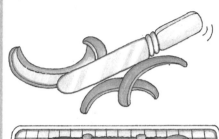

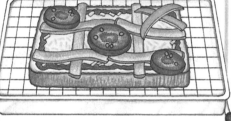

5 Slice the tomato and place in some of the squares to represent noughts.

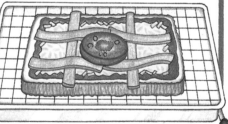

7 Place the pizza under the grill and cook it for about 3–4 minutes until well heated through and the cheese has melted.

Savoury Nests

You will need:

Food:
8 thin slices bread
butter
2 eggs
2 tablespoons milk
50g cheese
1 tomato
2 spring onions (optional)
salt and pepper
sprigs of parsley

This makes eight Nests

Equipment:
non-stick bun tray
pastry cutters to fit the bun trays
fork and tablespoon
basin
grater
knife

Before you start ask a grown-up to set the oven to 200°C/400°F/Gas 6.

2 Break the eggs into a basin, add the milk and beat together.

3 Grate the cheese and add to the egg.

1 Use the pastry cutter to cut out eight circles from the bread. Butter each circle and press it buttered side down into a bun cup.

4 Finely chop the tomato and spring onion and add to the egg mixture. Add the salt and pepper and beat the mixture well with a fork.

6 Meanwhile very finely chop the parsley.

7 When the cups are cooked, leave them to cool for a minute or two. Then ask a grown-up to remove the cups from the bun tray. Sprinkle them with the chopped parsley and serve at once.

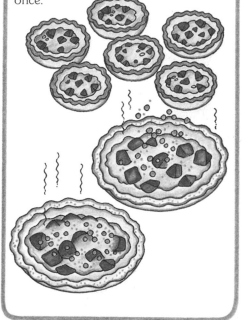

5 Spoon a little of the mixture into each bread cup. Ask a grown-up to bake the cups in the oven for 20 minutes so that they are set in the centre.

Popular Puddings

Home-made Summer Fruit Ice Cream

You will need:

Food:
350g raspberries or strawberries
150ml double cream
1 tablespoon sugar

This makes enough for four people

Equipment:
sieve
2 basins
wire whisk or fork
tablespoon
polythene container

1 Rub the fruit through a sieve into a basin.

2 Place the cream and the sugar in the second basin and whisk until soft peaks form. Do not make the cream too stiff or it will be waxy when frozen.

3 Mix the sieved fruit into the whipped cream. Spoon into a polythene container and place in the freezer or the frozen food compartment of the fridge. Leave to freeze solid.

If the ice cream has been stored for some time it may need to be taken out of the freezer to soften a little before serving.

99

Orange Crunch Creams

You will need:

Food:
½ packet chocolate chip cookies or your
  favourite chocolate flavoured biscuits
1 tablespoon flaked almonds
1 large orange
300g plain yoghurt

This makes four Crunch Creams

Equipment:
polythene bag
rolling pin
knife
tablespoon
4 glass dishes

1 Break the biscuits into pieces and place in the polythene bag. Hold the top of the bag and lay it on the work surface. Crush the biscuits by rolling over the bag with the rolling pin. Mix the almonds with the crushed biscuits.

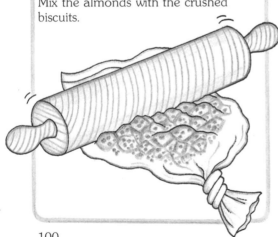

2 Peel the orange and remove all the pith. Break the orange into segments and cut each segment into four pieces.

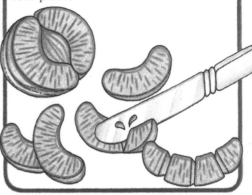

3 Place a tablespoon of yoghurt in the bottom of a small glass dish. Next add a spoonful of crushed biscuits and then a spoonful of orange. Top this with another spoonful of yoghurt and one of biscuits.

4 Repeat stage 3 with the other three glass dishes.

Gooseberry Layer Sundae

You will need:

Food:
280g can gooseberries
8 gingernut biscuits
50g hazelnuts
8 scoops ice cream

This makes four Sundaes

Equipment:
polythene bag
rolling pin
basin
knife
tablespoon and ice cream scoop

Before you start, ask a grown-up to open the can of gooseberries.

1 Place the gingernut biscuits in the polythene bag. Hold the bag closed and lay it on the work surface. Crush the biscuits by rolling over the bag with the rolling pin. Tip the crumbs into a basin.

2 Very finely chop the hazelnuts and mix in with the crushed biscuits.

3 Place spoonfuls of the gooseberries in the bottom of all four sundae dishes. Top this with a spoonful of nuts and biscuits and a scoop of ice cream.

4 Repeat these layers in all the sundae dishes and finish off by sprinkling with the last of the nuts and biscuits.

101

Ice Cream Sandwiches

You will need:

Food:
1 family block ice cream
1 packet thin wafers
chocolate vermicelli
1 tube Smarties
1 packet fruit pastilles
hundreds and thousands

This makes 12 Ice Cream Sandwiches

Equipment:
knife
2 plates
serving plate

2 Cut the wafers to fit the blocks of ice cream and place a wafer on each side of each slice.

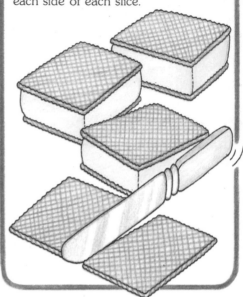

1 Cut the ice cream into 12 slices 1·5cm thick.

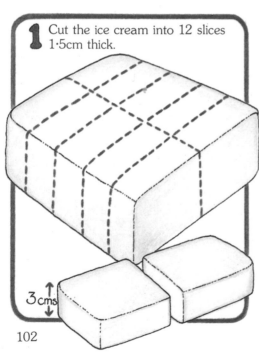

3cms

3 Sprinkle the chocolate vermicelli on to a plate. Holding one of the sandwiches between your finger and thumb, dip each side into the vermicelli. Repeat this for a second and third sandwich.

102

4 Press Smarties on to the sides of three more of the sandwiches.

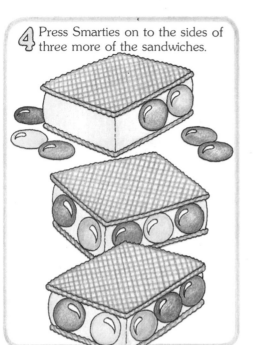

5 Press fruit pastilles round the sides of three more sandwiches.

6 Sprinkle the hundreds and thousands on to another plate and dip the sides of the remaining three sandwiches in this.

7 Arrange all the sandwiches on a serving plate and serve at once.

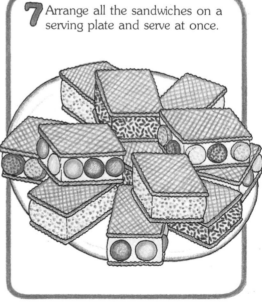

Ice Cream Nosegay

You will need:

Food:
4 scoops ice cream
small piece of angelica
small packet milk chocolate buttons
small tube Smarties

This makes four Nosegays

Equipment:
ice cream scoop or tablespoon
knife
4 paper bun cases

1 Place one scoop of ice cream in each paper case.

2 Cut the angelica into thin strips about 2cm in length.

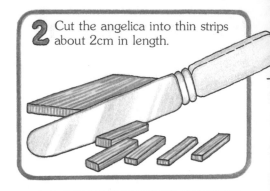

3 Arrange the chocolate buttons and sticks of angelica alternately round the edge of the scoop of ice cream and press into place.

4 Place different coloured Smarties above the angelica sticks and arrange some more in the centre of the nosegay. Press into place and serve at once.

104

Knickerbocker Glory

You will need:

Food:
1 small can raspberries
1 small can fruit cocktail
2 fresh pears
1 block Raspberry Ripple ice cream
raspberry Dessert Topping
2 milk chocolate flakes, cut in pieces
2 tablespoons flaked almonds

This makes four Knickerbocker Glories

Equipment:
knife
tablespoon
4 tall glasses

Before you start ask a grown-up to open the cans of raspberries and fruit cocktail.

1 Peel and halve the pears. Remove the cores and cut the pears into small pieces.

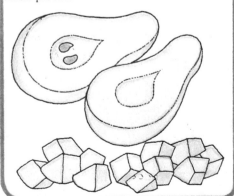

2 Place a spoonful of raspberries and juice in the base of each glass. Top this with a spoonful of ice cream and shake on a little Dessert Topping.

3 Next add a spoonful of fruit cocktail, some chocolate flake and some almonds. Add another spoonful of ice cream.

4 Finish off with the chopped pear, a third scoop of ice cream, Dessert Topping, chocolate flake and nuts. Serve at once.

105

Ice Cream Clown

You will need:

Food:
vanilla ice cream
1 pineapple ring
1 ice cream wafer
1 glacé cherry
2 raisins
a little raspberry Dessert Topping

This makes one Clown

Equipment:
ice cream scoop or round pastry cutter
knife
flat dish

1 Take a scoop of ice cream and place on a flat dish. If you do not have a scoop cut a 3cm slice of ice cream and cut out a round shape with a pastry cutter.

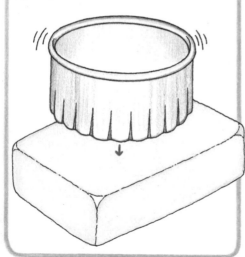

2 Cut the pineapple ring in half. Make two small cuts on the inside of the two halves so that they will open up a little more.

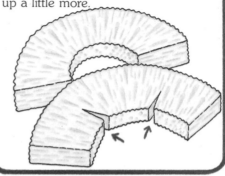

3 Place one of the half rings up against the ice cream so that it forms a ruff round the clown's neck. Place the second half on top of it.

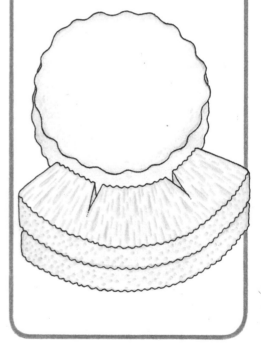

4 Cut the wafer into a tall triangular shape with a rounded top. Push the bottom edge into the ice cream on the side opposite to the ruff to form a hat.

5 Place the cherry in the centre of the ice cream to form the clown's nose. Use raisins for the eyes and make a mouth with a line of raspberry Dessert Topping. The Topping can also be used to make rosy cheeks.

6 Serve the clown before he melts!

Clock Pudding

You will need:

Food:
1 can peach slices
1 packet peach Instant Whip or Angel
  Delight
600ml milk
one 20cm sponge flan base
one glacé cherry
angelica or hundreds and thousands

This makes one Clock Pudding

Equipment:
basin
wire whisk or fork
knife

Before you start ask a grown-up to open the can of peaches.

2 Using the milk, make up the Instant Whip or Angel Delight as directed on the packet.

1 Drain the peaches very well and cut each slice into two along the slice.

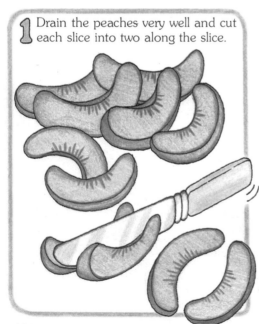

3 Place the sponge flan on a plate and spoon the prepared Instant Whip or Angel Delight into it. Smooth over the top with a knife.

108

4 Use the peach slices to make up the 12 numbers on a clock face. Cut the peaches into bits if you need to. Try Roman numerals if the curves of ordinary numbers are too difficult.

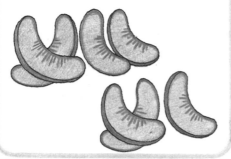

5 Put the numbers in place.

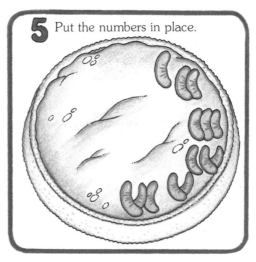

6 Place the glacé cherry in the centre and cut the angelica up to make the hands of the clock. If you do not have any angelica you can mark in the hands with a line of hundreds and thousands.

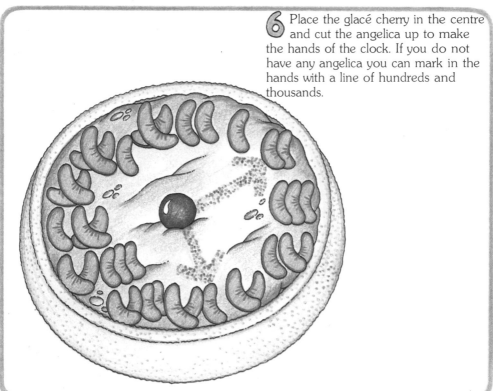

Yoghurt Picture Puddings

You will need:

Food:
2 oranges
500g plain yoghurt
2 tablespoons honey
chocolate or caramel Dessert Topping
raspberry or pineapple Dessert Topping
raisins and nuts

This makes enough for four Picture Puddings

Equipment:
knife
basin
4 glass bowls

1 Peel the oranges. Remove as much of the white pith as possible and break the oranges into segments. Cut each segment into small pieces. Place in a basin with any juice that runs off.

2 Add the yoghurt, honey, raisins and nuts and stir until well mixed. Spoon into individual glass bowls.

3 Decorate with Dessert Topping. For example, draw the outline of a boat with the chocolate topping and draw sails using raspberry topping, or draw the outline of a crown in caramel topping and the velvet headpiece using pineapple topping. Try thinking of other pictures to draw.

Fruit Crumble Pudding

You will need:

Food:
100g plain flour
50g butter
100g brown sugar
25g chopped nuts (almonds, hazelnuts,
  walnuts or unsalted peanuts)
500g plums
3 tablespoons water

This makes enough for four people

Equipment:
mixing bowl
tablespoon and knife
1 litre pie dish

Before you start ask a grown-up to set the oven to 180°C/350°F/Gas 4.

1 Place the flour in the mixing bowl. Cut the butter into small pieces and add to the bowl. Rub the butter into the flour with the tips of your fingers until the mixture resembles fine breadcrumbs.

2 Stir in 50g of the brown sugar and the nuts.

3 Wash the plums, cut them in half and take out the stones. Place the plums in the bottom of the pie dish and sprinkle with the rest of the sugar and the water.

4 Cover with the crumble mixture and ask a grown-up to bake the crumble in the oven for about 40 minutes.

111

Caramel Pears

You will need:

Food:
5–6 fresh or canned pear halves
4 tablespoons soft brown sugar
4 tablespoons Rice Krispies
50g butter

This makes enough for four people

Equipment:
knife
basin
shallow ovenproof dish

Before you start, ask a grown-up to open the can of pears and set the oven to 200°C/400°F/Gas 6. Peel fresh pears if you are using them.

2 Mix the sugar and Rice Krispies in the basin and then sprinkle over the top of the pears.

1 Cut the pears into wedges and place in the bottom of the dish.

3 Dot with butter and ask a grown-up to bake the dish in the oven for 30 minutes.

Marie Antoinette Cake-and-apple Pudding

You will need:

Food:
300g fruit cake
1 large cooking apple
1 large egg
300ml milk

This makes enough for four people

Equipment:
knife
small pudding basin
fork
measuring jug
1 litre pie dish

Before you start, ask a grown-up to set the oven to 190°C/375°F/Gas 5.

1 Cut the cake into thin slices about ½cm thick.

2 Cut the apple into quarters and cut out the centre core. Next peel the apple and cut into thin slices.

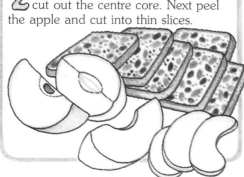

3 Grease the pie dish by rubbing a piece of buttered greaseproof paper over the bottom and the sides. Arrange the slices of cake and apple in layers in the dish, starting and ending with the cake.

4 Break the egg into a basin and break it up with a fork. Add the milk and continue mixing with the fork. Pour this mixture over the cake and apple. Leave to stand for half an hour.

5 When the pudding has been standing for half an hour, press all over the top with a fork. Ask a grown-up to bake it in the oven for one hour.

113

Apricot Cheesecake

You will need:

Food:
8 digestive biscuits
50g butter
50g sugar
250ml milk
$\frac{1}{2}$ packet vanilla Angel Delight
225g cream cheese
16 apricot halves, fresh or canned

This makes enough for six people

Equipment:
polythene bag and rolling pin
2 basins
wooden spoon and tablespoon
wire whisk or fork
16cm loose-bottomed cake or flan tin

Before you start, ask a grown-up to soften the butter and open the can.

2 Place the biscuit crumbs in a basin and mix with the butter and sugar.

3 Tip this mixture into the cake or flan tin and press down evenly all over the bottom.

1 Place the digestive biscuits in the polythene bag. Hold the top of the bag and lay it on the work surface. Crush the biscuits by rolling over the bag with the rolling pin.

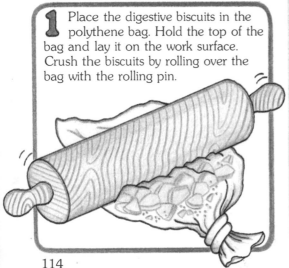

4 Place the milk in a basin and sprinkle on the Angel Delight. Beat in with a wire whisk or fork.

6 Spoon the mixture on to the biscuit base and place in the fridge to set.

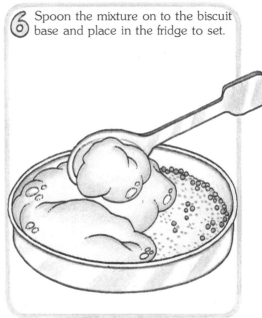

5 Beat the cream cheese with a wooden spoon to soften it and stir in the Angel Delight.

7 Just before serving, top with the apricot halves, placing them cut side down.

Chocolate Log

You will need:

Food:
125ml double cream
$\frac{1}{4}$ teaspoon vanilla essence
1 tablespoon sugar
16–18cm long chocolate swiss roll
chocolate cake decorations

This makes one Chocolate Log

Equipment:
basin
teaspoon
tablespoon
wire whisk
fork

2 Cut the swiss roll in half lengthways and spread one of the flat surfaces with some of the cream. Put the two halves of the swiss roll back together. Put the roll on a serving plate.

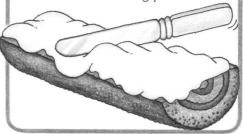

3 Spoon the rest of the cream all over the swiss roll. Spread with a fork and when the cream is evenly distributed over the cake make ridges in the cream by running a fork along the length of the roll. This gives the effect of tree bark.

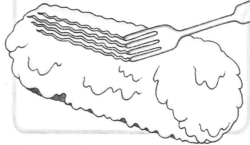

1 Pour the cream into the basin and add the vanilla essence and sugar. Beat with a whisk until the cream is stiff enough to stand up in soft peaks. Be careful not to beat for too long or the cream may curdle.

4 Sprinkle with chocolate cake decorations and place in the fridge to chill for an hour before serving.

116

Party Time

Train Salad

You will need:

Food:
1 stick celery
3 lettuce leaves
piece of cucumber 7cm long
25g cream cheese
$\frac{1}{4}$ teaspoon curry powder or paprika
  pepper
salt
2 large or 3 medium radishes
1 new carrot
1 piece cheese 7cm × 4cm × 3cm

This makes one Train Salad

Equipment:
knife and teaspoon
dinner plate and cup
2–3 cocktail sticks

2 Roll up the lettuce leaves and cut into thin strips. Arrange on either side of the track to represent grass.

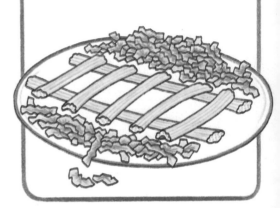

1 Cut the leafy head off the stick of celery and then cut it lengthways into long thin strips. Place two of these long strips on the plate as rails and cut the others up to make the sleepers of the track.

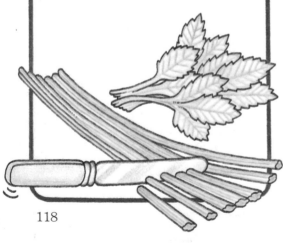

3 Cut the piece of cucumber in half along its length. Scoop out the seeds with a teaspoon and throw these away.

4 Put the cream cheese into a cup. Add the curry powder or paprika and the salt and mix well together with a spoon. Spread this mixture along the hollowed out halves of cucumber and press the two halves back together again. Keep a little bit of cheese to use to stick on the funnels.

5 Cut off the ends of the radishes and cut each radish into two thick slices for the wheels.

7 Cut the carrot into one 2cm length and one 1cm length and stick to the top of the engine with the remaining cream cheese to make the funnel and steam valve.

2cm   1cm

6 Push a cocktail stick through one end of the cucumber and thread a radish wheel on to each side. Do this again for the remaining wheels and stand on the celery track.

8 Stand the piece of cheese on end at one end of the cucumber engine to make the cab.

9 Place on the table ready for your meal.

119

Sausage Rolls

You will need:

Food:
small packet (215g) frozen puff pastry
flour
8 skinless sausages
mustard or tomato ketchup (optional)
milk

This is enough to make eight large or 16 small Sausage Rolls

Equipment:
rolling pin
knife
pastry brush
non-stick baking tray

Before you start ask a grown-up to set the oven to 220°C/475°F/Gas 7. Thaw the frozen pastry.

1 Sprinkle a little flour on the working surface and roll out the pastry to make a shape about 38cm × 24cm.

24 cms
38 cms

2 Place the sausages in two evenly-spaced rows down the length of the pastry. Spread a little mustard or tomato ketchup over each sausage, if you want to.

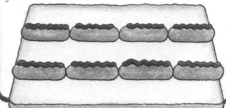

3 Cut the pastry down the centre and across between the sausages. Brush the edges of the pastry with water. Roll the pastry over each sausage, sealing the edges firmly together. Place on the baking tray making sure that the joins are underneath.

4 Brush with milk and ask a grown-up to bake the sausage rolls in the oven for 20 minutes so that the pastry is golden brown in colour.

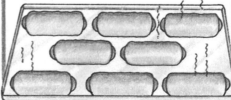

To make smaller sausage rolls cut each roll into two pieces before cooking

Snowy Mountain Dip

You will need:

Food:
175g cottage cheese
2 tablespoons sour cream or yoghurt
$\frac{1}{2}$ teaspoon caraway seeds
salt and pepper
$\frac{1}{2}$ small cauliflower
1cm long piece of cucumber
4 sticks celery

This makes one Snowy Mountain Dip

Equipment:
sieve
basin
tablespoon
teaspoon
cup
knife

1 Sieve the cottage cheese into a basin and mix in the sour cream.

2 Crush the caraway seeds by pressing them against each other with a teaspoon in a cup. Add them to the cream cheese mixture with salt and pepper.

3 Cut the cauliflower into small florets. Cut the cucumber in half and then into sticks. Cut the celery sticks into three and then cut lengthways into sticks.

4 Spoon the cream cheese and caraway mixture into a pile in the centre of a plate. Surround it with cauliflower florets and then with alternate piles of cucumber and celery sticks.

Rower's Boat Race Dip

You will need:

Food:
$\frac{1}{2}$ cucumber
175g cream cheese
2 tablespoons peanut butter
1 tablespoon milk
2 small carrots
4 sticks celery

This makes two Boats

Equipment:
knife
dessertspoon
basin
fork
large plate

1 Cut the cucumber in half lengthways. Scoop out the centres and keep the cucumber halves to one side.

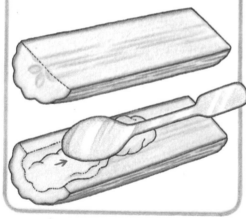

2 Chop the centre pieces of cucumber and place in the basin with the cream cheese, peanut butter and milk. Mix to a smooth paste with a fork.

3 Peel and slice the carrots into 18 rounds.

4 Cut any leaves off the sticks of celery, then cut each stick lengthways into four strips. This will produce 16 oars. Place the cucumber halves on a large plate with plenty of space between them, as boats.

5 Spoon the cream cheese and peanut butter mixture along the insides of the two boats.

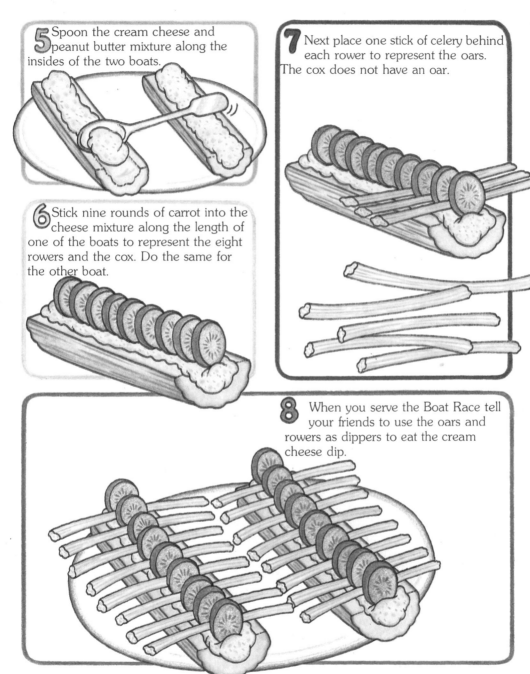

6 Stick nine rounds of carrot into the cheese mixture along the length of one of the boats to represent the eight rowers and the cox. Do the same for the other boat.

7 Next place one stick of celery behind each rower to represent the oars. The cox does not have an oar.

8 When you serve the Boat Race tell your friends to use the oars and rowers as dippers to eat the cream cheese dip.

123

Cheese and Herb Straws

You will need:

Food:
100g plain flour
pinch of salt
50g butter or margarine
50g cheddar cheese
1 teaspoon mixed herbs
1 egg

This makes about 30 Straws

Equipment:
sieve
mixing bowl
knife
grater
teaspoon
rolling pin
one fluted pastry cutter 9½cm across
one fluted pastry cutter 7½cm across
non-stick baking tray

Before you start, ask a grown-up to set the oven to 200°C/400°F/Gas 6.

1 Sift the flour and salt into the mixing bowl. Cut the butter or margarine into small pieces and add to the flour. Rub the fat into the flour with your fingertips until the mixture looks like breadcrumbs.

2 Grate the cheese and add to the flour mixture with the herbs. Stir together.

3 Break the egg into the mixture and mix first with a knife and then with the fingers to form a ball of dough.

4 Sprinkle flour on the work surface and place the ball of dough on it. Roll out the dough to about 0·5cm thick and cut out two circles with the $9\frac{1}{2}$cm cutters. Cut the centre out of the circles with the $7\frac{1}{2}$cm cutters. Carefully place the two pastry rings on the baking tray.

6 Press the trimmings from the pastry rings together and roll out again. Cut into 10cm $\times \frac{1}{2}$–1cm strips and place on the baking tray with the other straws. Ask a grown-up to bake the straws in the oven for about 15 minutes until they are golden in colour.

5 Cut the rest of the pastry into strips 10cm long and $\frac{1}{2}$–1cm wide. Place on the baking tray.

7 Leave the straws to cool and store in an airtight tin.

8 To serve, carefully push bundles of straws through the pastry rings.

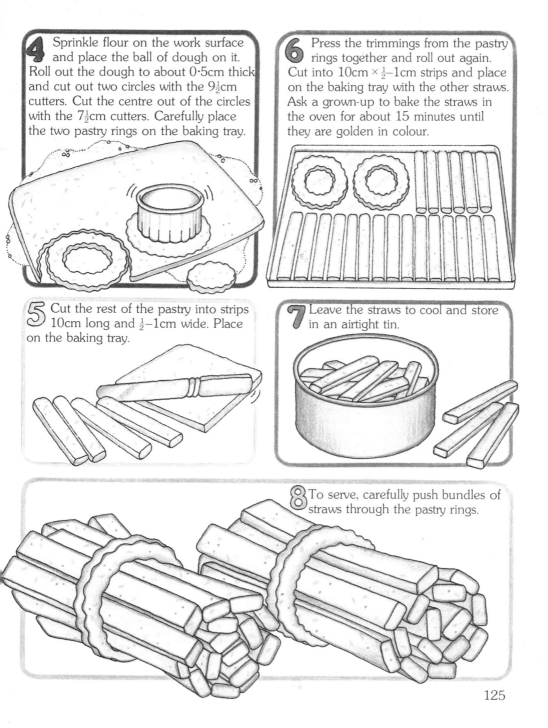

125

Cowes Regatta

You will need:

Food:
100g cheddar cheese
1 carrot
2cm piece cucumber
2 tablespoons salad cream or
  mayonnaise
salt and pepper
8 slices French bread, cut along the loaf
butter
2 tomatoes
2 slices processed cheese

This makes eight yachts in the regatta

Equipment:
grater
basin
tablespoon
knife
8 cocktail sticks

1 Grate the cheddar cheese, carrot and cucumber into a basin.

2 Add the salad cream or mayonnaise and the salt and pepper. Mix everything well together.

3 Butter the slices of French bread – these are the yachts.

4 Spread a little of the cheese and vegetable mixture on to each slice of bread.

126

5 Slice the tomatoes. Discard the rounded ends and place a slice on each yacht.

6 Cut each processed cheese slice in half and then cut each half into long triangles.

7 Thread each cheese triangle on to a cocktail stick to make a sail and stick one sail into the centre of each yacht.

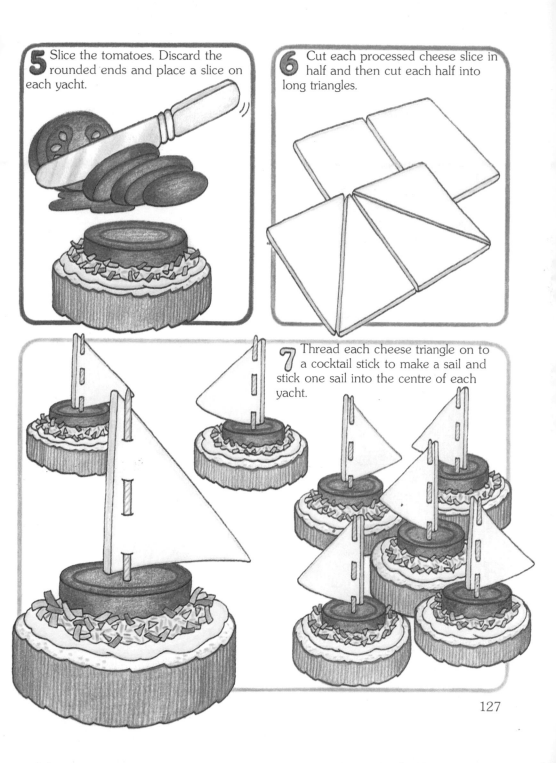

Party Hedgehogs

You will need:

Food:
150g Edam cheese
6 hot dog sausages
100g seedless grapes
small jar cocktail onions
4 oranges

This makes four Party Hedgehogs

Equipment:
knife
40–50 cocktail sticks

1 Cut the Edam cheese into small squares and cut each hot dog into about 4–5 pieces.

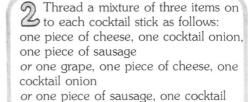

2 Thread a mixture of three items on to each cocktail stick as follows:
one piece of cheese, one cocktail onion, one piece of sausage
or one grape, one piece of cheese, one cocktail onion
or one piece of sausage, one cocktail onion, one grape

3 Place the oranges on a large plate with plenty of space between them and stick 10–12 filled cocktail sticks into each orange.

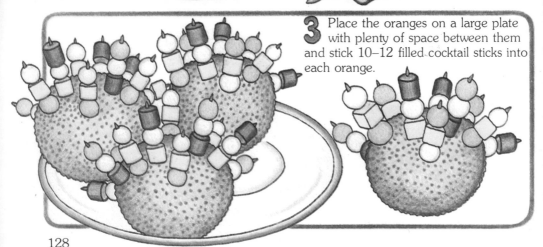

Tomato Cocktail

You will need:

Food:
600ml tomato juice
2 lemons
2 teaspoons Worcestershire Sauce
4 sprigs of mint

This makes enough for four Tomato Cocktails

Equipment:
measuring jug
knife
lemon squeezer
teaspoon
4 cocktail sticks

2 Squeeze the juice from one of the lemons and add to the tomato juice with the Worcestershire Sauce. Chill in the fridge for one hour.

1 Measure the tomato juice in a measuring jug.

3 Cut the other lemon into eight slices. Stir the tomato cocktail and pour into four glasses. Thread two slices of lemon, with a sprig of mint in the middle, on to each cocktail stick and place one on top of each glass.

Junior Pimms

You will need:

Food:
300ml cold tea
1 capful lime juice
3 capfuls orange squash
300ml lemonade
1 orange
1 lemon
1 apple
4 sprigs mint
ice cubes

This makes enough for four Junior Pimms

Equipment:
large jug
knife

Before you start, ask a grown-up to make 300ml weak tea. Leave it to go cold.

2 Cut the orange and lemon into slices. Core the apple and cut it into thin slices.

3 Add the fruit to the jug of tea and squash. Pour on the lemonade and add sprigs of mint and ice cubes.

1 Pour the tea, lime juice and orange squash into a jug and place it in the fridge with the bottle of lemonade to chill for one hour.

Blackcurrant Punch

You will need:

Food:
1 apple
4 cloves
2 capfuls blackcurrant squash
$\frac{1}{4}$ level teaspoon cinnamon
200ml water
400ml apple juice

This makes enough for four glasses of Punch

Equipment:
large saucepan

1 Stick the stalks of the cloves into the apple and place the apple in the saucepan.

2 Add all the remaining ingredients. Ask a grown-up to heat the mixture in the pan until it starts to steam. The mixture should not boil.

3 Leave the mixture to stand for 10 minutes. Drink it warm or leave it to cool and serve with cubes of ice.

131

Savoury Sandwich Cake

You will need:

Food:
1 large unsliced loaf
3 hard boiled eggs
cress
3 tablespoons mayonnaise
100g cooked chicken meat
50g sweetcorn
100g cheddar cheese
150g butter
1 tablespoon chutney
4 spring onions
75g cream cheese
a little milk
200g liver sausage
4 gherkins
25g cornflakes

This makes one Sandwich Cake

Equipment:
knife
tablespoon
5 basins
grater
wooden spoon
rolling pin
polythene bag

Before you start ask a grown-up to hard boil the eggs and to help you cut off all the crusts from the loaf, and slice the loaf into six slices along its length.

1 When the eggs are cool, shell them and chop finely in a basin. Mix in the cress and two tablespoons of mayonnaise.

2 Very finely chop the chicken and place in a basin with the sweetcorn and a tablespoon of mayonnaise. Mix well together.

3 Grate the cheddar cheese. In a basin, beat 50g of butter with a wooden spoon to soften it and mix in the cheese and the chutney.

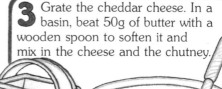

132

4 Finely chop the spring onions and mix in another basin with the cream cheese. Add a little milk if the mixture is very stiff.

5 Beat the rest of the butter with a wooden spoon in another basin and mix in the liver sausage to make a liver pâté.

6 Spread one slice of the loaf with the egg mixture and cover with a second slice of bread. Spread this with the cream cheese mixture and cover with another slice of bread. Spread this with a third of the liver pâté mixture, keeping the rest for the outside. Slice the gherkins very finely and arrange on top of the liver pâté.

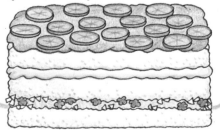

7 Cover with the fourth piece of bread and spread with the chicken mixture. Cover with another slice of bread and spread with the cheese and chutney mixture. Top with the last slice of bread.

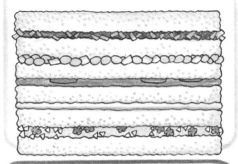

8 Spread the whole of the outside of the cake with the remaining liver pâté mixture, adding a little mayonnaise to the mixture if it is too stiff to spread easily. Put the cornflakes into a polythene bag. Hold the end closed and lay the bag on the work surface. Crush the cornflakes by rolling over the polythene bag with a rolling pin, and sprinkle the crumbs all over the cake.

Ice Cream Cabin

You will need:

Food:
100g almond marzipan
2 family blocks ice cream
soft chocolate ice cream
2 packets chocolate fingers
icing sugar
chocolate vermicelli

This makes one Ice Cream Cabin

Equipment:
knife
rolling pin
serving plate
tablespoon

1 Cut off a square of marzipan and use to shape a chimney.

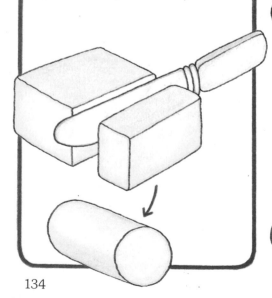

2 Sprinkle the work surface with icing sugar and roll out the remaining marzipan to 0·5cm thickness. Cut out a door and two windows.

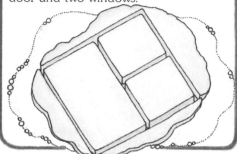

3 Place the two family blocks of ice cream one on top of the other on a serving plate.

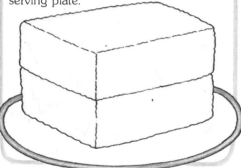

4 Press the door and windows on to one end of the cabin.

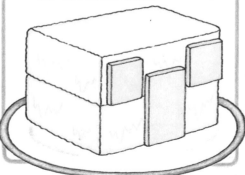

5 Arrange the chocolate fingers upright round the rest of the ice cream to form the log cabin walls.

6 Scoop spoonfuls of soft chocolate ice cream on to the top of the cabin and shape into a roof.

7 Sprinkle with chocolate vermicelli to look like thatch and press the chimney in place.

135

Spring Butterfly Cake

You will need:

Food:
250g icing sugar
125g butter
a few drops of red food colouring
one round sponge cake
2 tablespoons desiccated coconut
coloured sugar or hundreds and
  thousands

This makes one Butterfly Cake

Equipment:
wooden spoon
sieve
basin
knife
dessertspoon
2 candy striped straws

1 Beat the butter in the basin with a
wooden spoon until soft and
creamy.

2 Sift half the icing sugar into the
basin and beat again. Sift in the
remaining sugar and continue beating
until the mixture is very smooth and
creamy.

3 Add the food colouring a drop at a
time, adding only enough to turn
the icing pink.

4 Place the cake on a board and cut
in half.

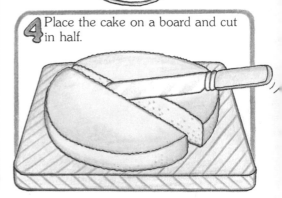

5 Turn each half round, placing the curved edges together.

6 Spread the butter icing all over the sides and the top of the butterfly.

7 Sprinkle with the coconut to give a furry look. Place one straw down the centre of the cake for the body.

8 Sprinkle the coloured sugar or hundreds and thousands to make patterns on the wings. Cut the second straw in half and push the halves into the cake to make antennae.

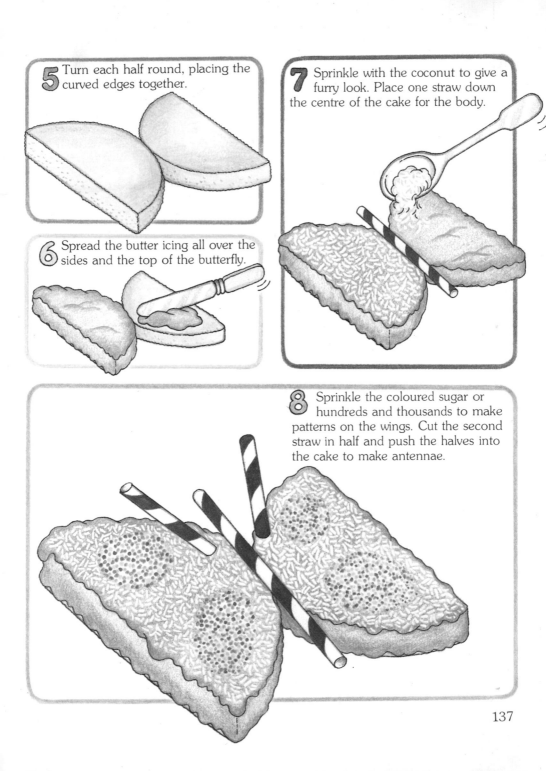

Castle Cake

You will need:

Food:
1 plain round sponge cake
6 tablespoons apricot jam
2 packets sponge fingers
1 packet marshmallows

This makes one Castle Cake

Equipment:
tablespoon
knife
flat serving plate
7 sticky labels and 7 cocktail sticks
coloured crayons

3 Cut the rounded tips off the ends of about 1½ packets of sponge fingers. Stand the fingers round the outside of the cake with the cut end on the plate and the flat side pressing against the cake. Make sure that the fingers are touching each other.

1 Slice the cake through in half and place the bottom half on a flat serving plate. Spread with two tablespoons of apricot jam.

2 Replace the top half and spread the rest of the apricot jam all over the cake.

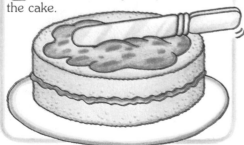

4 At one side of the cake leave a gap the width of three sponge fingers and instead of pressing these against the cake, arrange them to form a draw-bridge.

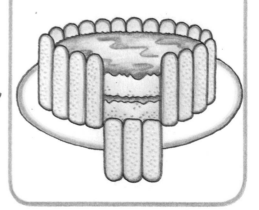

5 Cut the rest of the sponge fingers in half across and stand them up in a ring on the centre of the cake. Make sure that they are all touching each other so that they look like the keep of the castle.

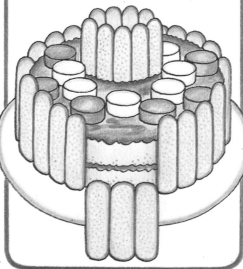

7 Cut six small and one large flag shapes out of the sticky labels and colour them with flag designs using your crayons.

6 Arrange the marshmallows on the top of the cake between the two rings of sponge fingers, arranging them carefully up to the edge of the cake over the entrance and drawbridge.

8 Stick one end of each small flag round a cocktail stick which has been broken in half. Place round the outside ring of sponge finger battlements. Stick one end of the large flag round a whole cocktail stick and stick this in the centre of the keep.

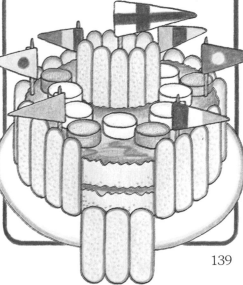

139

Home-made Sweet Shop

Orange and Chocolate Truffles

You will need:

Food:
100g Alpen or muesli mix
50g sugar
50g butter
50g milk chocolate
2 tablespoons orange juice
2 tablespoons drinking chocolate
  powder

This makes 16 Truffles

Equipment:
mixing bowl
knife
grater
tablespoon

2 Grate the chocolate into the mixture and add the orange juice. Mix well together and press down in the bottom of the bowl. Chill overnight.

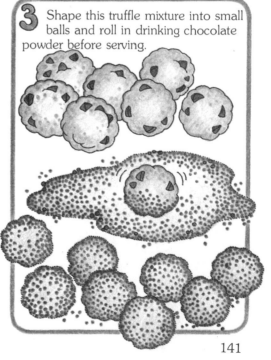

1 Mix the muesli mix and sugar in a bowl. Add the butter cut into small pieces. Rub the butter into the dry ingredients using the tips of the fingers.

3 Shape this truffle mixture into small balls and roll in drinking chocolate powder before serving.

141

Coconut Coffee Bonbons

You will need:

Food:
(for the bonbons)
50g butter
15g icing sugar
1 level tablespoon golden syrup
50g desiccated coconut

(for the coating)
1 dessertspoon powdered coffee
1 tablespoon icing sugar

This makes 16 Coconut Coffee Bonbons

Equipment:
basin
wooden spoon
tablespoon
dessertspoon

1 Place the butter in a basin with the icing sugar and beat with a wooden spoon until smooth and creamy.

2 Mix in the golden syrup and then the coconut. Place in the fridge to chill for two hours.

3 Shape the mixture into small balls. Chill again.

4 Make the coating by mixing the powdered coffee and icing sugar together in a basin. Roll the bonbons in the mixture just before serving.

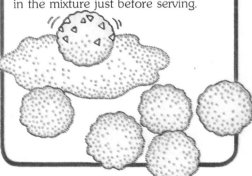

Cream Cheese Mints

You will need:

Food:
25g cream cheese
200g icing sugar
few drops peppermint essence

This makes about 16 Cream Cheese Mints

Equipment:
basin
dessertspoon
rolling pin
greaseproof paper
small pastry cutters

1 Place the cream cheese and sugar in a basin with the peppermint essence. Mix until smooth.

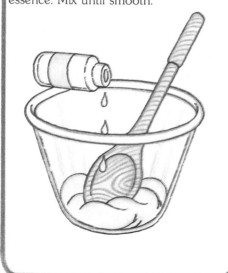

2 Sprinkle the work surface with icing sugar and place the cheese mint mixture on the top.

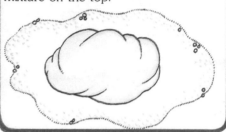

3 Sprinkle with more icing sugar and roll out. Use pastry cutters to cut out small rounds. Place the rounds on a piece of greaseproof paper sprinkled with icing sugar.

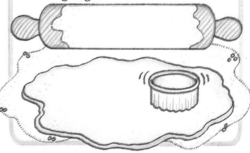

4 Press the trimmings together, roll out and cut out more mints. Leave to dry overnight.

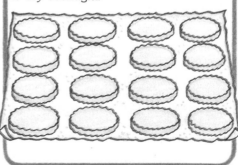

Stuffed Date Traffic Lights

You will need:

Food:
25 dates
75g cream cheese
grated orange rind
orange juice
25g icing sugar
1 packet Smarties

This makes 25 sets of Traffic Lights

Equipment:
knife
basin
teaspoon

2 Place the cream cheese in a basin and add the orange rind and a little orange juice. Mix well with a spoon and beat in the icing sugar.

3 Use this mixture to stuff the centre of the dates. Press a red, an orange and a green Smartie on to the stuffing to look like traffic lights.

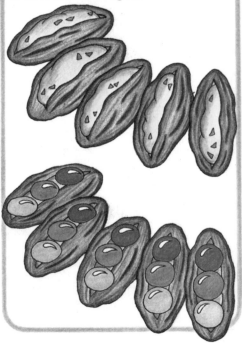

1 Slit the dates along one side and take out the stone.

Peppermint Creams

You will need:

Food:
400g icing sugar
1 egg white
lemon juice
peppermint essence

This makes about 25–30 Peppermint Creams

Equipment:
sieve
mixing bowl
wooden spoon
knife
greaseproof paper

2 Add the egg white, lemon juice and a few drops of peppermint essence. Mix well together.

3 Sprinkle the work surface with a little icing sugar and turn the peppermint cream mixture on to this. Knead well with your hands. After about 3–4 minutes shape the cream into a long sausage about 3cm high.

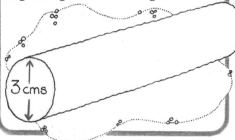

3 cms

1 Sift the icing sugar into the mixing bowl.

4 Cut the sausage into slices. Place the slices on a large piece of greaseproof paper and leave overnight to dry and harden.

145

Marzipan Fruit Basket

You will need:

Food:
225g almond marzipan
red, yellow and green food colours
icing sugar
angelica

This makes about 20 Marzipan Fruits

Equipment:
cocktail stick
small wicker or cane basket

1 Cut the block of almond paste into three portions and mould each portion into about twenty lumps.

2 Drop a small amount of food colour on to a lump and work the colour in with your fingers. Do this with all the lumps, making them either red, green or yellow.

3 Shape the different coloured lumps to make the fruit. If the marzipan begins to get sticky, sprinkle a little icing sugar over it.

4 Use some of the red marzipan to make strawberries. Prick all over with a cocktail stick to represent the seeds and make small leaves and stalks out of angelica and stick into the tops of the strawberries.

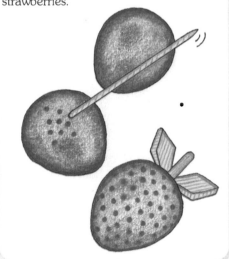

5 Shape some of the yellow marzipan into bananas.

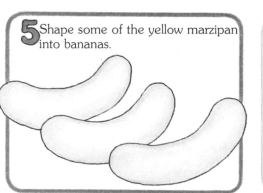

7 Shape red marzipan into round cherries. Roll out green marzipan into long thin sausages and use as stalks for the cherries. Join the stalks to make clusters of two or three cherries.

6 Shape some of the green marzipan into greengages and use angelica for leaves and stalks.

8 Shape yellow marzipan into lemons and prick all over with a cocktail stick to look like lemon peel.

9 Leave to dry overnight and then arrange all the fruit in the basket.

Cream Cheese and Fruit Balls

You will need:

Food:
25g dates
25g raisins
25g flaked almonds
100g cream cheese
$\frac{1}{4}$ teaspoon mixed spices
1 tablespoon cinnamon

This makes about 20 Cream Cheese and Fruit Balls

Equipment:
knife
basin
wooden spoon
saucer
20 cocktail sticks

2 Add the cream cheese and mixed spices and mix well together.

3 Place the cinnamon on a saucer. Shape the cream cheese and fruit mixture into twenty small balls. Roll in the cinnamon and put on a plate. Serve with cocktail sticks speared into each ball.

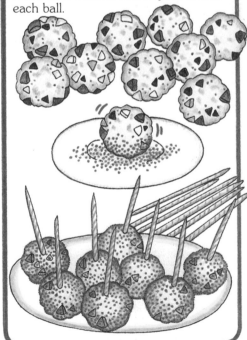

1 Finely chop the dates, raisins and almonds and place them in a basin.

Date and Nut Footballs

You will need:

Food:
100g dates
100g walnuts
50g soft brown sugar
2 teaspoons double cream or yoghurt
2 tablespoons icing sugar

This makes about 12 Footballs

Equipment:
knife
basin
teaspoon
tablespoon
sieve
plate

2 Add the soft brown sugar and cream or yoghurt and mix again. Place in the fridge to chill for two hours.

1 Very finely chop the dates and walnuts and mix well together in the basin.

3 Sift the icing sugar on to a plate. Shape the date and walnut mixture into small footballs and roll each one in icing sugar.

149

Sugar Animal Zoo

You will need:

Food:
50g golden syrup
500g icing sugar
1 egg white
3 food colours
silver balls
liquorice shoe laces
cornflour

This makes 10–12 Animals

Equipment:
mixing bowl
spoon
wooden spoon
3 basins
greaseproof paper

1 Weigh the bowl and then spoon the golden syrup into it until it weighs 50g more.

2 Sift 375g icing sugar into the bowl and add the egg white.

3 Mix well with a wooden spoon. Gradually add the rest of the icing sugar until the mixture feels like pastry.

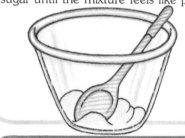

4 Divide the mixture into four equal parts and place three of the portions in separate basins. Add a few drops of your chosen food colour to the mixture, using a different colour in each basin, and knead well to distribute the colours evenly.

5 Shape lumps of the coloured mixture into elephants, bears, lions, crocodiles and snakes.

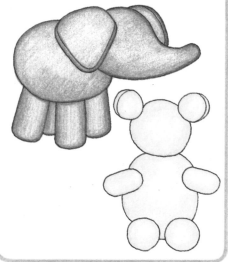

6 Use silver balls and liquorice shoe laces for eyes and tails.

7 Place the finished animals on a piece of greaseproof paper sprinkled with cornflour. Leave to dry overnight.

Coconut Puffs

You will need:

Food:
3 tablespoons desiccated coconut
few drops food colouring
1 egg white
20 marshmallows

This makes 20 Coconut Puffs

Equipment
jam jar with lid
basin
fork

1 Place the coconut in the jam jar with the food colouring. Replace the lid and shake the jar until the coconut is well coloured.

2 Place the egg white in a basin and beat well with a fork.

3 Dip each marshmallow in egg white and then in the coloured coconut. Make sure the marshmallows are well covered in coconut. Leave to dry for 2–3 hours and serve.

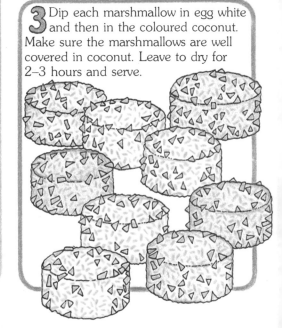

Coconut Ice

You will need:

Food:
50g cream cheese
200g icing sugar
75g desiccated coconut
a few drops red food colouring

This makes about 14–16 pieces

Equipment:
basin
tablespoon
shallow metal tin
knife

1 Place the cream cheese and icing sugar in a basin and mix together until smooth and creamy.

2 Add the coconut and mix again.

3 Spread half the mixture in a 12cm square on the tin and place in the fridge for 30 minutes.

12cms

4 Mix the remaining coconut ice with a little red food colouring. Spread over the top of the white layer and return to the fridge for 30 minutes. Cut into squares to serve.

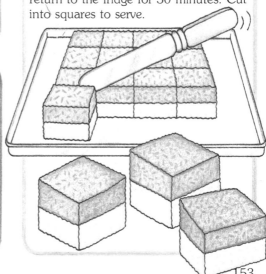

Nut Truffles

You will need:

Food:
25g walnuts
25g almonds
150g cake
100g butter
1 dessertspoon syrup
100g icing sugar
15g cocoa powder
2 tablespoons chocolate vermicelli

This makes 24 Nut Truffles

Equipment:
knife
grater
basin
wooden spoon
sieve

1 Finely chop the walnuts and almonds and rub the cake through a grater.

2 Cream the butter in a basin with the wooden spoon and beat in the syrup until the mixture is smooth and creamy.

3 Sift in the icing sugar and beat to a smooth cream. Add the nuts, cake crumbs and cocoa and mix to a stiff paste. Place in the fridge to set.

4 Shape the mixture into small balls and roll in chocolate vermicelli.

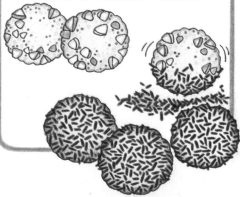

Chocolate Cheese Truffles

You will need:

Food:
100g cream cheese
250g icing sugar
50g cocoa powder
50g glacé cherries
chocolate vermicelli

This makes 16 Truffles

Equipment:
basin
sieve
tablespoon
knife

1 Place the cream cheese in the basin. Sift in the icing sugar and cocoa and mix until smooth and creamy.

2 Finely chop the cherries and add to the chocolate mixture. Place in the fridge for two hours.

3 Shape the truffle mixture into 16 small balls and roll in chocolate vermicelli. Leave to dry for at least two hours or overnight.

155

Easter Eggs

You will need:

Food:
250g almond marzipan
125g icing sugar
1 tablespoon hot water
few drops food colouring
chocolate vermicelli
coloured sugar strands

This makes about 16 small Easter Eggs

Equipment:
sieve
basin
wooden spoon
10–12 cocktail sticks
coloured silver paper
small bowl or serving dish

2 Sift the sugar into a basin and add the water. Mix to a smooth paste.

3 Using cocktail sticks dip about five or six of the eggs into the icing.

1 Shape the almond paste into about 16 small egg shapes.

4 Roll in chocolate vermicelli and place on some foil to dry.

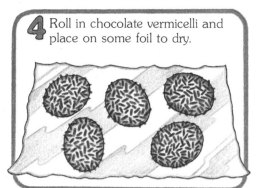

6 Roll these in coloured sugar strands.

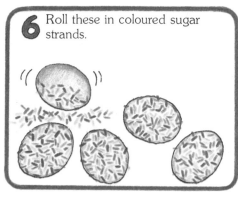

5 Mix a little of your chosen food colouring with the icing and dip five or six more of the eggs into the coloured mixture.

7 Wrap the remaining eggs in coloured silver paper.

8 Arrange in a small bowl to serve.

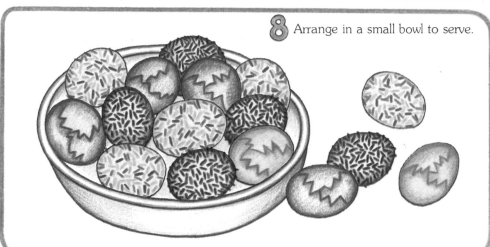